HOW WE
LIVE NOW

HOW WE LIVE NOW

MAKING YOUR SPACE WORK HARD FOR YOU

REBECCA WINWARD

RYLAND PETERS & SMALL
LONDON • NEW YORK

Senior designer Megan Smith
Senior commissioning editor
Annabel Morgan
Picture research Jess Walton,
Christina Borsi and
Isabel de Cordova
Production manager
Gordana Simakovic
Art director Leslie Harrington
Editorial director Julia Charles
Publisher Cindy Richards

First published in 2021 by
Ryland Peters & Small
20–21 Jockey's Fields
London WC1R 4BW
and
341 E 116th Street
New York, NY 10029

www.rylandpeters.com

Text, design and photographs
copyright © Ryland Peters &
Small 2021

10 9 8 7 6 5 4 3 2 1

ISBN 978-1-78879-183-0

A CIP record for this book is
available from the British Library.

Library of Congress CIP data
has been applied for.

Printed and bound in China

CONTENTS

INTRODUCTION

Whether you're a home owner or you're renting, whether you're young or old, whatever your preferred style, and whatever type of property you live in, chances are you sometimes wish your home could be a little bit bigger, or a little bit more practical, or a little bit more stylish.

Space is often the biggest issue for many of us. It's not uncommon to feel, after living somewhere for a few years, that you've outgrown your place - whether that's because your family has some new members (or you've made another change: perhaps you've started your own business or taken up a new hobby), or simply because you've accumulated more belongings. But whether the hassle of moving just doesn't appeal, you adore the location or the actual bricks and mortar of where you live now or you simply can't afford to stretch your finances to pay for a larger house or flat, it's worth considering how to make your space work harder for you so that you can stay put and be happier about it.

This book isn't so much an instruction manual on exactly what to do in a step-by-step way, rather a guide to the general principles of maximizing every inch of your home. Ultimately, it's a process that will be unique to every person and every property - but the way of evaluating the space and the creative thinking that is needed to perfectly combine aesthetic and practical considerations is a constant.

I hope not only to offer you a broad outline of how to go about creating a home that you simply love to live in, but also to inspire you to come up with your own innovative solutions to balancing your own particular circumstances, needs and budget. Happy homemaking!

1 FLEXIBLE SPACES

LIVING

In an ideal world (or, more specifically, home), we'd have enough square footage to enjoy our lives without limitations. Guests would have a comfortable spare room to sleep in, and children would enjoy a dedicated play area with the sort of toy storage that makes it easy for them to both play and tidy away independently. In reality, most of us occupy fairly modest homes and are frequently challenged by how much we are able to fit within our four walls.

But we don't have to resign ourselves to living in chaos, constantly frustrated by space limitations. With a little thought and some savvy choices, compact spaces can work hard. One of the easiest ways to do this is to consciously design rooms to be multifunctional: a kitchen-diner, a landing-cum-home office, a living room that can convert from playroom to party pad.

When it comes to combining functions, let common sense be your guide. A dining area is best located close to the kitchen, for example, while a reading nook or home office should ideally be situated away from a raucous play area or the high foot traffic of a hallway; and a space for painting or messy play is not ideally combined with a living space featuring expensive or difficult-to-clean soft furnishings. The key to success is to look at each and every part of your home carefully and decide which functions might suit the space best.

As every home's layout is different - and every household's needs are different, too - there won't be one successful, easily identifiable magic solution that works for us all. But there are some general principles that will help you achieve the best possible results in any property, and create interiors you truly love to live in.

WELCOMING LIVING SPACES

There are plenty of 'dos' when it comes to creating a friendly and welcoming living area, and quite a few 'don'ts', too. We've all been in a badly laid-out living area where the sofa/couch sits slap bang in front of the TV (or even worse, a blank wall) and there are no seats positioned opposite each other, which is really what's needed for a sociable chat, whether that's with family or friends. So how best to make the most of your space?

A pair of sofas facing each other is ideal for creating a convivial mood, though some modern rooms can be too narrow for this to work properly. If you can't manage this layout, even without a coffee table in the middle, try to arrange an armchair or two so they're facing the sofa/couch, even if they're positioned slightly at an angle. The more compact the design, the more likely you'll be able to achieve this. Therefore, look for lighter, sleeker shapes on slender legs rather than broad, squat designs. If at all possible, don't arrange your furniture around the TV set – try to position this off-centre or slightly to one side so it doesn't dominate the space.

If a coffee table would take up too much space, opt for side tables (or even a nest, from which occasional tables can be pulled

SOFA SO GOOD Don't assume you must have a three-piece suite in your living room. One comfy sofa/couch, plus a selection of other seating such as rockers, cocktail chairs or stools, creates a flexible area for everyone (right).

KEEP ON DISPLAY!
If your style mantra is 'less is more', up the cosiness factor using different textures and surfaces rather than filling the space with decorative objects.

YOU'RE WELCOME You've probably seen the horror of a matchy-matchy interior, where all the furnishings are in the same style and colour, and the curtains match the cushions – it feels claustrophobic, right? Change things up with a variety of contrasting textures and meaningful artwork and decorative collections, and your home will be infinitely more welcoming. The good news is that a relaxed, eclectic style is much easier to keep looking its best, because artfully empty, picture-perfect rooms look tired more quickly than a laid-back style that's a bit more 'lived-in' (opposite and right).

out when required). Just make sure that each chair has a tabletop placed within arm's reach so that people can put down their cup or glass instead of leaving it on the floor, where it will inevitably get kicked over. Don't forget to include table lamps or floor lamps, positioned either side of the sofa/couch where they can also act as reading lights.

Also consider the flow through and around a space – not just in terms of everyday comfort, but also for entertaining. Work out a furniture layout that allows you mingling space – whether that's by pushing furniture to the edges of the room or being able to fold up pieces to take up less space (such as gateleg tables and folding chairs).

PICTURE PERFECT Gallery walls can elevate your decor to the next level, but it can be tricky to know where to start. The easiest option is to go for a grid of same-sized images, or a set of frames sold together for this purpose with instructions on how to hang them in the intended configuration (below left). However, if you want to create a unique display, it's worth creating paper blanks the same size as your collection of frames, and arranging them on the wall first using masking tape to keep them in position, before fixing the pictures to the wall. Start with the largest, then fill in with smaller ones, while aiming to create a sense of balance (left and below).

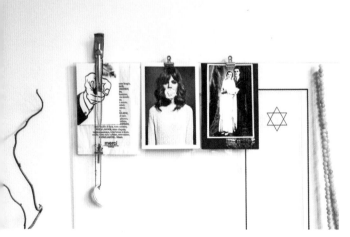

TAKE INSPIRATION

Giving a display a sense of coherence is important. In this room, the collection is united by its restricted colour palette, evident in both the artworks and the framing.

ZONING OPEN-PLAN SPACES

Nowadays, so many of us live in open-plan spaces that must combine several different functions. The secret to success here is to plan the layout so that it not only allows an easy flow of movement through the room but also works in both an aesthetic and practical sense. For example, if you're creating a study area in a living space, then position all the necessary storage close to the desk, eliminating the need to constantly cross the room (or go next door) to access files, the printer and stationery supplies.

You'll create a much more considered vibe by ensuring there's decorative coherence between two zones within the same area. For an open-plan living space plus dining area, you could arrange two matching sofas opposite each other, ideally

with a coffee table in between, for a pleasingly symmetrical sitting zone at one end of the room, then place the dining table and chairs at the other end, so that the room's two purposes are clearly defined. Rugs are an excellent way of demarcating these different zones – place one at the heart of the seating area, then use another to anchor the dining table or your desk. Lighting also has a role to play here – suspend low pendants over a dining table, then opt for wall lights and reading lights alongside the sofa/couch in the living area.

Large bookcases or shelving units work well as room dividers, but make sure the piece is stable by fixing it either to the wall or the floor (especially if you have young children). Ceiling-hung curtains can also be used to divide spaces and conceal specific areas (you might want your desk or work area out of sight in the evening, for example). They're a flexible solution, as they can be drawn back when not required.

If you have a kitchen and living room in the same space, you may want more of a physical

ADDING DEFINITION Make sense of an open-plan space with some structure created by the layout of furnishings – cluster comfy chairs around a coffee table (maybe on a rug that's warm and welcoming underfoot), and you've clearly demarcated the living area (opposite). Another idea is to hang a pendant light (or a whole row of them) along the length of a dining table, which will ensure the stage can easily be set for both casual family dinners and formal entertaining at the mere flick of a switch (above).

DIVIDE AND CONQUER Not everyone likes their open-plan spaces to be entirely open – this can be a bit too lacking in cosy credentials for some people. If simply zoning by function isn't quite enough for you, then consider how you might use key pieces of furniture to divide the space up into different 'rooms', without actually breaking up the sight lines with solid walls. Glazed sliding doors, shelf units used as room dividers, folding screens and even just strategically placed sideboards/credenzas and sofas/couches can all help to create intimate, function-specific areas (this page).

barrier – a butcher's block, kitchen island or dining table – between the kitchen cabinets and the sitting area. If this isn't possible, angle your sofa/couch so that it faces away from the kitchen area and creates a sense of separation. If your front door opens directly into your living space, then some kind of screening will be invaluable – a stud wall painted to match the walls would be the sleekest option, but a tall screen can be a great alternative if you don't fancy DIY.

When it comes to decorating, you'll want to create a sense of harmony by ensuring there are visual links between the two different spaces. Paint the whole area the same colour for a more seamless finish. Similar materials, colours and styles of furniture and other accessories will all offer a sense of decorative cohesion, as does a single type of flooring.

TAKE INSPIRATION
A huge amount of functionality can be squeezed out of a tiny footprint. This minuscule apartment (above) fits kitchen, diner and living space into one modest room – and it works.

TAKE INSPIRATION
Open-plan doesn't have to mean minimalist. A more relaxed, even cluttered, and family-friendly aesthetic can work just as well.

LEVEL BEST If your open-plan living area has a double-height ceiling, then a mezzanine level is a good way to obtain extra usable space. Mezzanines are sometimes used for bedrooms, but this is usually only in properties for two (this page). This is owing to the trickiness of the privacy situation – when you want to go to bed but the rest of your household wants to spend time in the living area, arguments could ensue. In a family home, these platforms are better utilized as home offices, reading areas or teen hangouts (opposite).

PUTTING UP GUESTS IN YOUR LIVING ROOM

» With rents and property prices being what they are, spare rooms are becoming less common, but this doesn't rule out having guests to stay. You will, however, have to give some careful thought to how things might work.

» Think about how you can help guests – who don't know your home – feel more comfortable. For example, a lamp within reach of the sofa bed will avoid stubbed toes in the dark on the way back from switching off the light, while a nightlight in the hallway makes night-time trips to the bathroom less stressful. Similarly, try to provide things they might need so that they don't have to ask or go poking about in the small hours – a glass of water, a towel or an extra blanket in case they get cold.

» A sofa bed instead of a standard sofa/couch in the living room is the only major change you need to make. But do be sure to position it in the right place, in order that minimal rejigging of the layout is required when converting the space from living to guest room. If you also pay attention to privacy and practical considerations, your friends will certainly thank you. If your living room is a through route to another part of the house (say, if it's how you access the stairs, or you need to pass through from the hall on the way to the kitchen), then the addition of a strategically placed folding screen or curtain could spare some blushes.

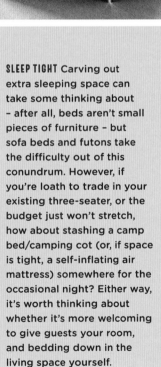

SLEEP TIGHT Carving out extra sleeping space can take some thinking about – after all, beds aren't small pieces of furniture – but sofa beds and futons take the difficulty out of this conundrum. However, if you're loath to trade in your existing three-seater, or the budget just won't stretch, how about stashing a camp bed/camping cot (or, if space is tight, a self-inflating air mattress) somewhere for the occasional night? Either way, it's worth thinking about whether it's more welcoming to give guests your room, and bedding down in the living space yourself.

HARD-WORKING STORAGE

While cabinet furniture takes up floor space, wall-hung storage allows the maximum amount of floor to be seen, and built-in storage helps to streamline an interior. Both these alternatives can make a room seem bigger, and there are plenty of useful and stylish options to consider.

Modular shelving is a great choice for anyone with limited square footage. It's entirely flexible, as it's made up of different configurations of shelving and other units, and when you move you can take it down and reassemble it in a new home. Contemporary designs can make a style statement in their own right, especially if you opt for a design classic such as the Vitsoe 606. Modular shelving doesn't have to be expensive, though – there are great designs available at many price points, including an IKEA version. And if you don't want to commit to a modular system, look for a wall niche or space that can accommodate two or three shelves and fix them on attractive brackets.

There are myriad other types of wall-hung storage out there, from wall-mounted TV stands to decorative shelving units – look for on-trend shapes and materials such as bamboo or brass. These can be a good alternative to artworks and make a good home for treasured personal items and pot plants.

If your living space is open plan, a fold-down kitchen table is visually unobtrusive yet will offer extra space for food prep and eating when needed. And then there are smaller solutions, too, such as wall-mounted hooks, pegboards and magazine racks (these are great for other things as well). Just be sure to use the right fixings for the wall type and the amount of weight you want the storage to hold – though remember it's always better to fix to solid walls if you can. Ask in a DIY store for fixings advice if you're uncertain.

EVERYTHING HAS A PLACE You literally can never have too much storage space, and one of the ways to best maximize capacity (without cluttering your home with a miscellany of cupboards, chests and boxes, is to build it into the fabric of the room (opposite). Painted to tone in with the walls, this type of storage becomes part of the backdrop to your decor, while secreting away all manner of things, resulting in a more harmonious ambience (and a better-organized life). Consider installing floor-to-ceiling cupboards/closets (keep them shallow if floor space is tight), shelves (floor-to-ceiling is also a good choice here) or even more unusual built-ins, such as banquette seating or an under-bed storage platform with lift-up hatches.

BLAST FROM THE PAST Vintage finds – or, if you're short on sourcing time, vintage-style pieces – can really inject some character into your space, as well as proving highly practical. Whether you choose a mid-century modular wall-hung unit, or repurpose wooden or wire crates as wall-hung shelves, or build a console table with crates as supports, you can add storage and display functionality to your home at quite a low cost (this page).

KEEP ON DISPLAY!
Rather than hanging artworks on the wall, why not display them on open shelves like these, along with a selection of books and decorative objects?

DOUBLE DUTY One of the easiest ways to make your interiors deliver more for you is to make sure furnishings are chosen that offer dual functionality – and furniture with storage capacity is one of the most straightforward choices you can make. Ottoman beds that have lift-up mattresses or standard storage beds with drawers, desks with integral shelving, coffee tables with compartments, sofas/couches with under-seat storage, armchairs with integrated bookshelves... there are plenty of clever designs that represent savvy buys, whether your home is compact, or you just want to have the benefit of as many storage options as possible (left and opposite).

DUAL-PURPOSE FURNITURE

Any pieces of furniture that do double duty or can be folded away out of sight when not in use will help your living space work harder for you. Popular choices include storage ottomans used as coffee tables (they can double as additional seating, too) and low stools that can also serve as side tables. Look out for coffee tables that offer integrated storage, such as bookshelves or magazine racks. Flat-topped storage chests or trunks are another canny choice, as they can double as a coffee table. Nesting tables may not strictly be dual-purpose, but they do allow you to fit in two or even three tables for the floor space of one.

For a dining area or kitchen where you're short of space, look for drop-leaf or gateleg tables with sides that fold down when not in use, leaving you with a piece of furniture that can do double duty as a console or side table. If you have more room, look at extendable tables where you can add and

subtract a leaf as desired; the extending leaf can usually be stored under the tabletop (or under the bed) when not in use. Folding or stackable chairs are another easy way to immediately free up floor space, as is the classic butler's tray table on a stand – simply fold away under the bed when it's not needed.

Storing things under the bed isn't a new idea, but storage or lift beds or those with drawers in the base take the concept a step further and allow access to storage space under your mattress for bedding, household linens or out-of-season clothes. If you are likely to be putting up visitors overnight, look for armchairs that pull or flip out into a single bed and ottomans that perform the same trick. And if you've got the space, you can opt for that old favourite, the sofa bed or futon.

SMALL SPACES

» If your pad is teeny tiny, life will be so much easier if you plan your interior thoughtfully and live in an ordered way. Effective storage, so that you can stash everything away (and regular clear-outs, to combat any hoarding tendencies) is a must if you're going to keep things looking tidy rather than literally and visually cluttered.

» When it comes to the decor, the usual advice is to choose a pale colour scheme and neutral flooring, but darker schemes can also be very striking if they are carried through with conviction. Opt for sleek lines, plain surfaces and natural materials to keep the feel calm and spacious. One savvy trick is to paint the walls, skirting/base boards and woodwork/trim the same colour to create the illusion of uninterrupted space.

» And, of course, maximize light in whatever way you can, whether that's through careful consideration of window dressings (avoid anything dark or heavy, or that screens the window at all times) or strategic placement of floor and table lamps. Mirrors bounce light into dark corners and can stop a space feeling poky.

» Aside from style considerations, the key to success is the proportions of the pieces you choose. Make sure you buy suitably scaled furniture - measuring out your space, hunting down something of the right dimensions and even marking out the footprint of the piece on the floor using masking tape before you commit. Don't try to squeeze in large pieces just because you can physically fit them in. If a room looks cramped, it will seem even smaller.

KEEP IT SIMPLE Once the more practical issues, such as choosing furniture of the right proportions and making sure that routes through spaces are unhindered have been considered, one of the essentials to getting it right in a small home is the style you choose. A pared-down, simple aesthetic will always help to maximize a sense of space (this page and opposite). Think simple, plain blinds or curtains, neutral colour schemes (you can always give things a lift with a dash of colour here or a spot of contrasting texture there) and furnishings with sleek lines.

RELAXING

It's no secret that modern life is often stressful - many of us work long hours (perhaps with a lengthy commute), or are frantically juggling family commitments with paid work, as rising living costs push us to work longer and harder.

Then there's the impact of living in a hyper-connected world, where electronic devices enable us to access media any time and (almost) any place, which makes it more difficult to switch off. Additionally, as more of us work from home these days, there can be a blurring of boundaries, which makes it trickier to escape the pressures of our jobs and take time out for ourselves.

But solitude is essential for allowing the brain space needed to rest and recharge - it's not just technology that works best if you periodically turn it off, then on again - so it's important to create quiet areas of the home that support this necessity. We need spaces in which we can unplug and spend down time, both completely on our own, and also alongside others;

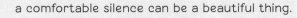

a comfortable silence can be a beautiful thing.

Bedrooms are the most obvious example of a space that needs to promote relaxation - sufficient good-quality sleep being critical to our wellbeing - but quiet corners in living areas (or a book nook or other spot tucked in elsewhere) and bathrooms also deserve attention as spaces that can promote wellness through relaxation.

The basic principle for designing these spaces holds true, whether you're talking about a whole room or just a corner of one: try to consider all the senses when creating a restful ambience. Visual calmness is of course important, but sound, smell and touch are also key.

ARE YOU SITTING COMFORTABLY?

SOFT OPTIONS A selection of cushions of varying types (firmer ones for support, squishier ones to sink into luxuriously) will up the comfort factor on sofas and armchairs – don't forget to add a throw or two for chilly evenings (above left and right and opposite). Such snuggling is not just a pleasingly cosy sensory experience, but a chance to keep heating costs down!

It's a no-brainer: for optimal relaxation your seating should hit the sweet spot between soft and supportive. If an existing sofa/couch and chairs don't quite meet the mark but you don't have the budget for replacements, consider upping the comfort factor by replacing the cushions. Vary the size and firmness, so that anyone who sits there will be able to get the seat feeling just right.

If you don't have a sofa/couch (perhaps you're just about to move into your first unfurnished place) or your existing one is too tired and saggy to be spruced up with new cushions, then put in some proper research before you buy new (or second-hand – look at local selling sites and eBay). After all, a sofa/couch is a key piece, both practically and decoratively speaking.

If you're investing in new upholstered furniture, make sure you measure up carefully, taking into account not only the dimensions of your living area but also the access to it.

TAKE INSPIRATION
Placing your comfy seating around a rug will deliver a cosier feel underfoot, and this sort of arrangement creates a pleasing visual focus, too.

NICE LEGS In a small room, opt for sofas and armchairs with visible legs; you can see the floor underneath each one, which creates the illusion of more space (this page and opposite). That said, you might prefer to choose the possibility of the hidden storage space offered by a sofa with a pelmet!

Surely there's nothing more annoying than ordering the perfect armchair only to find it won't fit through the sitting room door. If access is tight, explore low-armed or low-backed options or modular designs that are delivered in sections. And if space is in short supply generally, don't try to cram in the biggest sofa/couch possible. It will dominate the room and make it feel crowded. In a tiny space, consider a love seat or something with a slim profile and small footprint – like a vintage Ercol sofa or armchair (it's amazing how much space can be saved by a design with narrow arms).

Just as with beds, it's important to try out sofas/couches and chairs before you buy, so make sure that you (and anyone else in your household) get to 'test drive' the shortlisted options. This will enable you to make an informed choice and ensure maximum comfort levels. Finally, on a practical note, if you have pets or kids (or are just likely to accidentally knock over a drink in the vicinity), then look for upholstery that can be spot cleaned, or pieces with washable loose covers/slipcovers. Leather is a super-practical solution as it simply wipes clean (look for a coated finish).

Do consider investing in a footstool so that you can put your feet up at the end of the day (a storage ottoman is a savvy choice), and also think about additional seating for when you have a full house – floor cushions, upholstered stools and little round pouffes are all a great idea.

PLUG IN Lighting schemes don't have to be about permanent, wired-in fittings. Experiment with table and standard lamps, candles and nightlights and even strings of decorative LED lights. You can add or remove these easily and move them around to find the right configuration for your space, without incurring an electrician's bill and the disruption caused by chasing cables into the walls (left and opposite). And if your aim is to create a hard-wired lighting scheme, it doesn't hurt to use lamps as a temporary measure to figure out where the fittings need to be installed, before you commit to the expense and upheaval.

LIGHTING FOR AMBIENCE

Different occasions call for different moods, and one of the quickest ways to set a mood is with a layered, flexible lighting scheme. Obviously, any scheme must be practical, offering illumination for activities such as reading, knitting or cleaning. But you'll also want to layer up other lights that create the appropriate atmosphere for relaxing and for entertaining.

One very quick way to ensure the right ambience at the flick of a switch is to fit dimmer switches instead of rockers – it's a simple job for a registered electrician and shouldn't mess up your decor either, as long as you choose similar-sized plates. This way you can dial down any central fittings when you want a more chilled mood, or dim fittings at one end of the room while keeping them bright at the other. Changing your bulbs can also have a dramatic effect. Opt for warm white LED bulbs to create a cosy ambience. Their cool white counterparts cast a harsh, clinical light, and won't feel welcoming or homely.

Don't forget table lamps. Not only do they throw additional light but they are also decorative items that bring interest and personality to a space. Vintage bases have eclectic charm, but there are literally hundreds of attractive lamps and shades out there. If you don't have enough surfaces, look for a freestanding reading lamp on a slender leg that can slot in either side of (or even behind) the sofa. For a dramatic effect, you can angle an adjustable reading light to highlight a favourite artwork or a display of treasured collectibles on bookshelves or a tabletop.

Twinkly nightlights will instantly give any space a festive, celebratory feel – just make sure any naked flames are not left unattended and are kept well away from anything flammable (battery-powered versions are best if you have kids or pets).

BRIGHTENING UP
DARK SPACES

» We all know the benefits of good natural light - it's an instant mood-enhancer, and makes any space seem more appealing. However, only the luckiest among us will be able to choose a home based on light levels. But that doesn't mean you have to put up with dark corners and dreary spaces; there are ways to maximize the natural light in your home. You can choose decor that will enhance a brighter ambience, and use the right lighting to compensate, too.

» Firstly, is there anything restricting the natural light from the windows? Are there bushes or climbing plants getting in the way? Do the windows need cleaning?

Perhaps the curtains/drapes or blinds/shades are blocking more light than necessary? Remove heavy drapes and pelmets and replace them with simple linen curtains or Roman blinds/shades.

» Replacing solid internal doors with glazed doors will help natural light flood into darker areas such as hallways, while strategically placed mirrors will bounce light around a room. Your decor will make a difference, too. Light colours on the walls and reflective surfaces (such as gloss paint on the woodwork/trim) will all give a space a brightening boost.

» While you might not want to opt for brighter bulbs in the ceiling and wall fittings (they can feel a bit harsh), try layering in some additional lighting. A table or standard lamp will enhance a dark corner - even better, put one in every corner of a room - while small floor-standing uplighters can wash light across ceilings and walls, and will subtly boost the ambient light levels.

STAND FIRM It's important to make sure lamps are positioned in places where they won't get knocked over – especially if you have small children or pets. Wall-mounted fittings of the kind that don't need their wires chasing into the wall can be a really good choice for busy family homes for this reason (opposite above and right). If you decide to include a standard lamp in your scheme, make sure it has a heavy base and is stable (opposite below and below).

TAKE INSPIRATION

Cut flowers perk up any room, but potted plants have longevity – and greenery like this can be just as beautiful, as well as offering health benefits.

PLANTS FOR A HEALTHY ATMOSPHERE

GO GREEN By bringing the outside in, you can add the power of the natural world to the restful ambience you're creating – nature is known for helping us rest and rebalance, so plants in the home can enhance your sense of wellbeing (above, left to right). If you're not green-fingered, ask in your local garden centre which plants might suit your space.

As they can help improve air quality, house plants are not just a great choice for aesthetic reasons but for health ones, too. Plants act as a natural filter, cleaning the air, absorbing toxins and producing oxygen. And they're firmly back in fashion – an essential for any room with pretensions to style.

However, whether you've got green fingers or are a complete gardening novice, a little thought should be put into your selection of greenery, depending on where it will live. For optimal air-purifying qualities, choose a mother-in-law's tongue (also known as the snake plant), peace lily or Boston fern, all of which absorb harsh chemicals such as carbon monoxide and formaldehyde, and are pleasingly low maintenance as well.

Great choices for a sunny windowsill include the houseleek, aloe, bead plant, dragon plant and variegated spider ivy, all of which are easy to grow. No direct sun in your space? Then look for an African violet, begonia, Swiss cheese plant, a philodendron or a common aspidistra, all of which will be content in a shady spot and don't need much watering either. If temperature levels fluctuate and the natural light isn't the best (in a hallway, for example), then you'll want to choose something hardy like a glossy Ceylon creeper, a dwarf mountain palm or a rubber plant.

Finally, ideal plants for bathrooms (which can be both cool and humid) include the striking silver inch plant, maidenhair fern and creeping saxifrage.

DECISIONS DECISIONS There are so many different types of plant available that making a choice can be dizzying. It's important to choose a plant that suits the light levels in your room, and also matches your level of gardening expertise (some plants require a fair bit of husbandry; if you're not much of a gardener, these ones probably won't be for you). Ask for or research air-purifying plants, which have the ability to counteract toxic emissions (this page and opposite)

LIVING WITH BOOKS

Book lovers may now have the space-saving option of e-readers, but many of us still relish the reassuring weight of an actual hardback or paperback in our hands – and a book collection (of whatever size) can not only be a very cherished possession but also bring an additional dimension to an interior's aesthetic appeal.

Fitted bookshelves are the obvious choice for book storage, but if space is tight, think creatively about where you put them. A wall-hung shelf above a doorway, for example, can be an excellent way to use 'dead' space that isn't ordinarily filled with anything. Wall niches or the alcoves either side of a chimney breast are traditional locations for built-in shelves, but if you don't have these, other storage options are worth considering. If you have a large library, a modular shelving system is an excellent and stylish solution, and it can be

dismantled and taken with you if you relocate. There are also lots of freestanding shelving options. Although these tend to be less flexible, they can be an attractive addition to a room and some can even act as room dividers (but make sure you fix them to the floor if you have pets or children).

As well as being vehicles for thoughts and knowledge, books can be decorative objects in their own right. Current reads can go on a coffee table. In addition, stack volumes under tables or benches, arrange them in empty fireplaces or awkwardly shaped alcoves or alongside ornaments on trolleys or in display cabinets.

SHOW SUPPORT If you have a lot of books, then their storage must be thought about carefully – not only will you need space but sturdy shelves are a must, as a large collection of books can accumulatively weigh rather a lot (above left and right and opposite).

RAINBOW COLOURS If you have a collection of books with brightly coloured spines, then one way to create visual impact is to order them by shade rather than by type or subject – this can be particularly striking if the room decor is neutral, whether it uses darker or lighter tones, as the colours will really pop (above and right). If you like the idea of books as decorative objects, but your collection doesn't really lend itself to this treatment, then you could consider covering them with patterned or plain paper (though admittedly, if you have hundreds this might be a bit of a tall order!).

RECYCLED PIECES AND VINTAGE FINDS

SUCH A CHARACTER One of the most appealing aspects of old pieces is their texture – there's no faking the beauty of original surfaces (above right and above). Replicas are great these days, but authenticity is better!

Vintage pieces and recycled materials can bring a great deal of character to any interior, no matter how small it may be. They're also an enduring interior design trend. A white-walled rental apartment is a great backdrop for a few carefully selected vintage finds, while recycled textures – wood, metal and glass – will bring warmth and visual interest to open-plan spaces.

Let's start with the walls. If you're in a new build that's sorely lacking in personality, you could clad the walls of the hall or the living space in reclaimed wood planking or wooden panelling

(this is also great for soundproofing, if you live somewhere with a lot of ambient noise). If the wood is painted and peeling, so much the better. However, if you prefer a cleaner, more neutral finish, sand it down, then wax or varnish the surface. Alternatively, paint the walls with a raw plaster tone to introduce warmth and texture. In an older property, scraping off layers of old wallpaper and paint can create an intriguing decorative backdrop to simple furniture and other accessories.

When it comes to vintage furniture, less is more: it's best to incorporate one or two pieces to avoid the flea market vibe (unless that's the look you're specifically going for!). Items that are versatile enough to slot easily into any scheme include a leather armchair, a vintage desk (perhaps teamed with a modern desk chair) or a 1970s sideboard/credenza to hold the TV or act as overflow storage for china and tableware. Keep everything else pared back and simple, and allow those pieces to introduce an eclectic feel.

Another option is to transform vintage pieces with a coat of paint to tie in with a more contemporary scheme. This works well with smaller pieces of storage – painting them all the same colour will unify different shapes, materials and eras. It's also possible to find furniture made from reclaimed materials. For many people, this offers the best of both worlds; texture and a sense of history are combined with clean modern lines.

TAKE INSPIRATION
Mixing the warm patina of rustic timber with sleeker finishes – paint, plastic, stone or steel – creates a wonderful contrast that can really lift a space.

PATIENCE IS A VIRTUE It can take time to find the right vintage piece – it has to be the perfect fit in terms of style, size and budget. There's nothing like a fortuitous find at a junk shop, but it's also a good idea to keep a wishlist on you (your smartphone's notes app is perfect for this exercise). Keep a note of all the items you're looking for, and when it comes to furniture, the dimensions of the space you'd like them to fit in, so that you can check a piece's suitability when you stumble across it (right).

PERSONALIZING A CHARACTERLESS RENTAL

» Even if you're only planning to stay in a rental for a few months, take time to inject a little of your own personality into the space. Chances are the interior will be neutral, and not exactly inspiring (sometimes not even practical), so you'll reap the dual rewards of having a cosier home that also suits your needs better.

» Firstly, what does your tenancy agreement say? If you want to make more significant improvements than new curtains, a rug or decorative accessories, then ask your landlord. If the change is easily reversible (like painting the walls) or will add value to the property, chances are you'll get a positive response.

» If you aren't allowed to paint, knock picture hooks into the wall or switch out kitchen cupboard doors, you can always inject your own sense of style with some easy decorative updates.

» Hang pictures using Command strips or hooks, or simply use masking tape to affix photos to the wall (for the ultimate in studio chic choose black-and-white prints and opt for black masking tape).

» Command hooks are also good for hanging storage in the kitchen, coat storage in the hallway or for fixing wire baskets to the wall.

» Stickers and decals can add a temporary decorative touch to walls, whether painted or tiled.

» Can't hang artwork or mirrors because it's against the terms of your lease? Choose larger options and lean them against the wall.

» Removable contact paper is ideal for customizing inexpensive furniture, changing up surfaces or kitchen cabinets or as temporary wallpaper (stick it to the wall and paint with blackboard paint, for a non-permanent blackboard wall).

» Cushions and throws can be found at low cost, but remember that bright colours often look cheap. If you're on a tight budget, stick to muted palettes and create interest by layering textures.

» Check out thrift shops and online auction sites such as eBay for quirky items that add character without breaking the bank.

CHERRY ON TOP Rentals can be frustrating, because often you're not allowed to make any significant changes to the decor itself. But if you can flip your thinking, you'll perhaps see that it's also a plus: as you don't have to worry about the underlying decoration, you can just focus on furnishing and accessorizing your space. Also, you can have fun trying out quirky decorative ideas to see how they work, without needing to commit to big changes that take significant time and budget (this page and opposite).

EATING AND ENTERTAINING

Mealtimes aren't just refuelling stops for humans; they have huge social and cultural significance, and the nourishment is certainly as much emotional as it is physical. As a result of a growing awareness of the importance of eating together, these spaces are being given more focus than ever before - and it seems unbelievable that we thought the TV dinner would mark the end of the dedicated dining area.

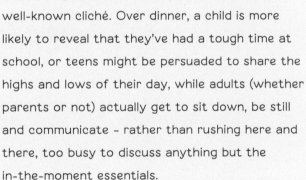

But over the years, many homes have been built without an obvious space for dining, leaving many of us with the challenge of carving out space for a dining table and chairs - but it's well worth meeting the challenge head-on.

Some might say the kitchen is the heart of the home, but you only have to look at where the most engaging conversations happen, and the dining table has a strong case to rival the

well-known cliché. Over dinner, a child is more likely to reveal that they've had a tough time at school, or teens might be persuaded to share the highs and lows of their day, while adults (whether parents or not) actually get to sit down, be still and communicate - rather than rushing here and there, too busy to discuss anything but the in-the-moment essentials.

Then there's the celebratory function. Memories are made over the dining table, when birthday candles are lit, and other important milestones and high days and holidays are toasted with friends and family. This is a part of the home that will always be important.

OPEN-PLAN KITCHENS

Open-plan kitchens are certainly appealing in the way in which they can make daily life more sociable – nobody has to separate themselves from the rest of the household to go and prepare a meal. They're also something of a space-saving option because you can fit more functions into a smaller area while still maintaining a sense of space and openness.

Having said that, there are a few considerations you'll need to heed if your kitchen is open plan. Appliances need to be quiet, to avoid having to tune out the washing machine's spin cycle while lying on the sofa drinking wine and watching a favourite film, for example. By the same token,

hob/stovetop extraction fans need to be both quiet and very effective – you don't want your soft furnishings smelling like last night's dinner.

With the usual layouts involving kitchen cabinets running along just one side of the room (maybe a little way along a second side, or, if you're very lucky, a peninsula unit, too), you'll need to cleverly maximize the available storage space. Make the space work harder by fitting splashback hooks and hanging rails, or by choosing compact pots, pans and bowls that nest together when they're not in use. And keeping kitchen work surfaces clutter free equals a calm, clear backdrop when you're entertaining or trying to relax.

CENTRAL PERK If there isn't room for an island unit in your kitchen, consider whether a good old-fashioned kitchen table could fit instead – though, of course, it's only the concept that is time-honoured, as modern designs work well, too (this page and opposite).

KEEP ON DISPLAY!
It's not a family kitchen without notes and pictures (even kids' artwork stuck up somewhere), though a noticeboard works just as well as the refrigerator.

BRING IT TOGETHER Open-plan spaces look best if there's a sense of coherence in the overall decorative scheme but discrete zones are obvious, too. Here, the use of the same materials – timber, concrete, iron – and the same utility-chic aesthetic gives this large kitchen-diner a harmonious feel, while the layout makes each area's function abundantly clear.

PRACTICAL CHOICES

Unless you've got deep pockets and plenty of time for housework and furniture care, you'll want to opt for surfaces and finishes that are easy-care, so that your interiors stay looking at their best without too much hassle.

Hard floors are undoubtedly best in areas that might get wet or messy – in the kitchen, bathroom, hallway and dining room (especially if you have children or pets). Vinyl, laminate and ceramic tile are among the most hard-wearing, affordable and easy-to-look-after choices. Solid and engineered wooden floors are warm and characterful, but are not quite as durable when it comes to water spillages or leaks, although solid wooden floors can be sanded down and refinished.

If you're painting anything – walls, kitchen cabinets or furniture – make sure you choose the right type of paint for the surface (and prepare that surface correctly before grabbing your paintbrush). You'll want a finish that stands up to soap and water, so try looking for a formula that is marketed as being particularly wear resistant or even stain-repellent.

Foil- or vinyl-wrapped kitchen cabinets are the option with the lowest price-point, and they are easy to care for because they're wipe-clean – but do try to buy the best quality you can afford for maximum longevity. It's better to avoid high-gloss finishes, as these tend to show scratches and fingerprints much more easily.

OVER THE THRESHOLD In a small open-plan space, it can work well to use the same flooring throughout, but there's also a practical argument for choosing tiles in the kitchen even if you're planning wood underfoot in the dining area. When done right, this makes for a striking decorative choice, too (this page and opposite).

BLANK CANVAS One style of kitchen unit that seems to work universally is the white, minimalist, handle-free aesthetic. Thanks to its neutrality, it can provide the ideal backdrop for a wide range of style choices, whether contemporary or historical. The heavy antique refectory table with benches shown here is a case in point.

PUT IT AWAY!
For the ultimate in practicality, only keep objects in daily use out on your worktops – put everything else away to reduce unnecessary washing and dusting.

Although solid wood might be a little more expensive, it is a timeless and versatile material. Wooden kitchen cabinets or dining tables can always be sanded and refinished to give them a new lease of life. Cheaper furniture with a veneer or laminate top can't be – so consider buying decent-quality pieces second-hand, and giving them a facelift for the best value longer term.

IT'S ALL ABOUT YOU 'Un-kitcheny' furniture and finishes will bring personality to what can be a sterile environment and make your kitchen feel more like a living space than a purely functional area (this page). Don't forget to add artworks, cookbooks and other decorative flourishes.

KITCHEN STORAGE

Out of all the rooms in the house, storage probably plays the most critical role in the kitchen. This space needs efficient, capacious storage like no other, to cope with everything from spices to tableware to the recycling bin. Having a home for everything really does make daily life so much more frictionless.

Most items can be housed in the conventional way, in wall-hung or undercounter cabinets. Kitchen designers have umpteen clever gadgets for maximizing cabinet space, from spinning carousels to pantry drawers. It makes sense to group objects together and keep them close to where they will be used – saucepans near the hob/stovetop, and tableware and glassware close to the sink and dishwasher. Items that are not used every day should occupy the less-accessible corners.

If the fitted cabinets in your kitchen don't provide quite enough storage for your needs, you'll be looking at pieces of unfitted or freestanding furniture. A dresser/hutch is always an attractive addition, as it showcases china as well as offering large storage cupboards, while glazed wall-hung cabinets look pretty filled with glassware. Open shelving allows easy access, so is ideal for items used on constant rotation such as mugs, coffeepots, glass tumblers and so on. It can also look very pleasing if you fill shelves with attractive, colourful packaging and other decorative pieces – jugs, vases, hand-crafted pottery bowls and the like.

HANG IT ALL If your kitchen cupboards are bursting at the seams, then squeeze in some additional storage space with rails and hooks. Make use of the splashback area (you can even get purpose-made wall-hung storage systems), and consider ceiling racks, too.

OPEN-MINDED Open storage is best for items in constant use; if you're a keen and busy cook, then it could suit your needs well. Take inspiration from professional kitchens and opt for hanging storage plus freestanding shelves and trollies that keep everything within arm's reach (left, right and opposite). Put storage boxes on casters to increase functionality – they're a great way of making use of the dead space under sideboards and tables (below left).

A trolley on wheels or butcher's block with shelves beneath is an excellent way of making additional storage space at the end of a run of cabinets. Stainless-steel catering units and shelving are another good option for frequently used items. And don't forget your walls either. Magnetic strips can hold knives near a food-prep area, while a slim metal rail fixed to the wall near the hob/stovetop is a good place from which to hang graters, ladles, sieves and all those other pieces of everyday kitchen paraphernalia.

KEEP ON DISPLAY!
Don't keep pieces for 'best'. Use your favourites daily, and keep them on open shelves, as seen here, where they can be appreciated as well as speedily reached.

FLEXIBLE DINING SPACES

A dedicated eating space is a must, even if you don't have a dining room, since there are times when a TV dinner or bowl of cereal balanced on your lap on the sofa just won't do.

Your main consideration is, of course, the dining table. Look at your kitchen and living room area – at the very least, can you squeeze in a small drop-leaf table and a couple of folding chairs? Another option to maximize a small space is to have banquette seating built in along the wall (great for incorporating storage inside, too!), and position a narrow table and any additional chairs next to it. This also works well in an awkward corner – think of an L-shaped banquette and a round table.

In general, opt for a round dining table if you can – it's the most sociable shape to sit at, since everybody is facing inward, and it's also possible to buy some quite compact designs, including some where the chairs fit around it perfectly, keeping the footprint to a minimum and the look sleek. If your dining area is long and narrow, hunt down a slimline table and maybe even plump for a bench or two rather than chairs, as these will tuck away neatly and unobtrusively when it's not dinnertime.

When space is so tight that you really don't have the option of a permanent dining area, how about a temporary one? Push the furniture back and put up a folding table and chairs for a dinner party or poker night, then simply put them away again afterwards (behind the sofa or under the bed are prime spots for storing such items when they're not in use).

TURN THE TABLES Match your table to your needs – refectory examples are great for big families, while couples who eat out a lot may only need a breakfast bar or small wall-hung design (left and above left).

SIZE DOESN'T MATTER A kitchen breakfast area is nice to have. It doesn't have to be big or fancy – a simple breakfast bar or small table will suffice (this page).

MADE TO MEASURE Built-in banquette seating is a win for those who need capacious storage provision in the kitchen – it's amazing how much you can stow away in the under-seat compartments (above). Consider other bespoke options for this space, too, and don't just get stuck in the standardized unit mindset, even if your budget is modest – you may be surprised at the value offered by a local carpenter. Even a single one-off piece, such as a dresser/hutch or sizeable wall shelf (right, above right and opposite), designed to fit the space perfectly, can make all the difference in terms of both practicality and aesthetics.

2 WORKING FROM HOME

WORKING

It's becoming much more common to work from home these days, thanks to employers coming around to the productivity benefits of flexible working, entrepreneurs setting up their own businesses and an explosion in the number of us working a side hustle - whether that's a spin-off from a hobby, a little freelancing on weekends or a second job (or even studying for a career change).

Even if nobody living under your roof brings work (of any description) home with them, the chances are that there will still be at least one member of the household who needs space for schoolwork, or for a hobby or - at the very least - a designated area that makes life admin easier and more efficient. You might be surprised just how much positive impact this can have on your ability to get to grips with a busy lifestyle.

Whether you've got enough square footage for a dedicated home office, a flexible study-cum-guest-room or just a desk slotted into the corner of the living area or kitchen, the same

rules apply to what makes the space practical and a pleasure to work in. The key is to think carefully about what would help you get your tasks done (or get those creative juices flowing), and build exactly the work zone to match those needs (and the needs of others who share your home). Then you just have to figure out a way of squeezing all that into whatever floor area you can spare!

Thankfully, there's a multitude of clever, space-saving furniture designs and storage solutions available nowadays - and with just a little creativity and thought, it's possible to put together a workspace that works for you, even if you're on a shoestring budget.

CREATING A FLEXIBLE WORKSPACE

TAKE A CHAIR If you're not planning to use an adjustable office-style chair, it's important to make sure that your chosen seat is the right height for your desk – if you're not comfortable, you won't be able to focus well (above left and right).

Not many of us have the square footage for a separate home office, and if this is true of your situation, then a dedicated workstation slotted into another room will be the only way to go. If you're smart about it, no-one will even notice that you're squeezing in an additional function to the space – either you'll have incorporated it seamlessly into the room's aesthetic, or you'll have come up with a clever way to keep it hidden away until required.

When space is at an absolute premium, look for a wall-mounted desk that drops down when required, and then folds up again to occupy as

little space as possible. Floating wall-mounted shelf desks are another option. Choose one with a cubbyhole or shelf below and you can store your laptop there when not in use.

If you've got a spare corner in the living or dining area, look for furniture that transforms when office space is required, such as a sideboard/credenza that becomes a desk by sliding the top forward, or a secretaire chest with a fold-down work surface (perfect for lovers of vintage style).

SImilarly, there are armoire offices, which are tall purpose-made cabinets with a pull-out keyboard shelf, and storage shelves above, with a spacious cupboard below to hold files and stationery supplies. These come in all sorts of different styles, from French shabby chic to mid-century modern, to match the rest of your decor. They're a great solution for awkward niches or an unused area in a hallway or entry. Alternatively, opt for a desktop on trestles, which is easy to remove and slide away under a bed or behind a door if you're planning to have a party.

Or why not hide your office in a built-in closet? Top-hung sliding doors (or a curtain) allow you to roll your chair under the desk when you're done, then put everything out of sight. If you already have a wall-mounted modular storage system with uprights and brackets, there may be a desk module available. Modular storage systems are ideal for creating a versatile work area that's tailored to your needs – and they're great for making the most of every inch of space, too.

PERSONAL EFFECTS Think about putting together a collection of decorative objects that contributes to the perfect work environment for your specific needs and tastes. Do black and white prints engender a calm ambience that ensures focus (right)? Or do you like to have a small library of books to hand? Perhaps a pinboard covered with clippings, photos and other curiosities will get your brain into the right zone for creative thinking? Don't forget to curate your collection – too many bits and pieces can be distracting, make it tricky to keep your desk clean and can also look cluttered.

KEEP ON DISPLAY!
Pictures don't have to be hung. Leaning artwork up against a wall (on a shelf, desk or even the floor) allows you to play around with the arrangement any time you want.

THE LONG GAME A built-in desk with a long run of work surface (whether it's straight or around a corner), and storage cabinets or shelves underneath, is a great choice both practically and aesthetically (opposite and right). The sleek lines of a desk with two or more workstations ensure that the room doesn't look like a corporate office, plus this type of design not only has the benefit of providing work space for multiple family members but also helps keep the central part of the room's floor area clear – which makes it a perfect solution for multifunctional rooms.

BUILT-IN DESKS

It almost goes without saying that built-ins are a great way to use every inch of space in a way that suits your needs perfectly – after all, they are bespoke. They're also a particularly good way to squeeze a workspace into an awkward or narrow room, because you're not constrained by standard widths when it comes to the work surface.

But while a professionally designed desk installation is a beautiful thing, you don't need a large budget or a lot of DIY skills to create your own. With some sturdy cabinets of matching heights (metal drawer units are ideal) and a length of work surface (reclamation yards can turn up some gems, such as old school chemistry lab worktops), you can have yourself a unique desk – just make sure the top is securely fixed to the wall, so that it can't be knocked off the cabinets that are supporting it.

SEE THE LIGHT In a more compact space, it's well worth carefully choosing furniture that gives a lighter aesthetic feel – such as a desk with a slim top and elegant trestle legs (left and opposite). Slender pieces give the illusion of more space, because they allow the eye to see through and around them, whereas heavy designs will fill the eye and can make a room seem fuller and smaller. However, this has to be a balancing act; cupboards and cabinets, which are essential for providing storage and streamlining the appearance of any clutter, are necessarily chunky. Pale colours, restricted colour schemes (such as the more-practical-than-it-sounds 'white on white' approach) and the use of sleek, even reflective surfaces (and clear glass or Perspex) can be useful tools for achieving balance.

TRESTLES AND FOLDING DESKS

With their sleek, leggy aesthetic, trestle desks score highly when it comes to style points, but they can be super-practical, too – storage shelves, hooks and holders are often incorporated into the trestles, and you can also find designs with adjustable height for the perfect ergonomic working position. Some trestle designs are made to be easily dismantled and packed away, which means they're ideal for small or multifunctional spaces where a desk needs to be a temporary feature (but do make sure you check, since the distinctive shape of trestle legs doesn't always indicate that functionality!).

It might take a little searching, but it's also possible to find folding desks that can be quickly and easily packed away under a bed, slid under a sofa/couch, or stood up inside a

TAKE INSPIRATION
Of course you'll need to make sure you've got enough room for your legs, but tucking a shallow storage unit under your desk (left) is a great way to carve out extra storage space.

built-in wardrobe/closet – and there are some with legs and tops that fold down flush with the wall when not in use. Other 'convertible' options include wall-hung drop-downs, gateleg-style desks, L-shaped designs where the right-angled part can be rolled back under the main desk top, and – if you really don't have any space for a proper desk – small folding tables that go over your lap while you're sitting on the sofa, or even in bed!

TASK LIGHTING FOR WORK AREAS

» Professionally designed interiors usually feature carefully formulated lighting schemes, but it's perfectly possible to do a pretty good job of improving on the basic central ceiling pendant by adding some well-chosen task lamps. Great news if you don't have the budget (or the time or the inclination) to pay an electrician to wire in new lighting and then a decorator to make good any damage.

» When adding lighting fixtures to a workspace, consider the positioning of each one carefully – you don't want to place lamps where their light will glare in your eyes or reflect in the computer screen. A central ceiling lamp with a bulb on a long flex/cord can be looped over a cup hook attached to the ceiling so that it illuminates your desk top rather than a central patch of carpet. Then layer up a variety of unfitted wall, standard and table lights to create a flexible and effective scheme that meets your needs. Table and standard lamps project zoned pools of light onto a work area and can also be decorative items in their own right, while directional task lamps can be angled to highlight artwork or decorative features, as well as to light up tasks such as reading, writing or household admin.

» If floor space is limited, then choose wall lamps with an external flex/cord with an integrated rocker. Fix one to the wall by your desk, plug it in and flick the switch. Plug-in lights can also be hung from a decorative bracket above a desk.

» Don't forget the fun stuff – string lights or even an LED neon light hung on the wall over the desk can quite literally brighten up a dull corner.

SWITCHED ON Lighting is so important for a comfortable and productive work environment, and following a few simple pointers makes it easy to get it right. Firstly, don't forget about natural light (left and below). Position your desk so that you're able to work in daylight, giving consideration to screen glare (if it's impossible to avoid, think about translucent blinds). Secondly, when you look at task lighting, don't just take into account position (aim to avoid shadow and reduce harsh reflections), but also specification – choose bulbs carefully in terms of strength and warmth (opposite below left).

LEARNING

Working at home is not just about adult work. For small children who have not yet started formal education, art and creativity are their way of learning about the world and experimenting with new-found skills. School-age kids will need somewhere to get down to their homework, as will teenagers. How best to allow for all these activities?

Small children will need a desk or table for art and craft activities - modelling, drawing, doing puzzles and imaginary play all require a wide, wipe-clean surface that's the right height. Provide them with such an area, and they'll spend many happy hours there. If you have space in the kitchen, it's the best place for a 'creation station', as generally kitchen surfaces are more impervious to paint and modelling material damage than the sitting room. If this isn't possible, look for a suitable location in a corner of your living space (as far as possible from your beloved velvet sofa) or perhaps on a landing or hallway just outside the kitchen door.

If you can fit them in, push two small tables together to make a longer run so that siblings or friends can create alongside one another. This will ensure there's plenty of surface area for drawing and painting, sticking and making, jigsaw puzzles and so on. Storage for art and craft supplies needs to be positioned close to hand. A mobile trolley is a great way to corral all these items together in one place and can be wheeled out of sight when the kids are in bed and you're eating dinner.

When the homework schedule starts in earnest, it'll be time to revamp your child's learning zone so that it's conducive to concentration and quiet study, as discussed overleaf.

THE HOMEWORK ZONE

When children start school, it's an excellent idea to create a dedicated study space where you can be on hand if they need help with their homework (or to nudge them into staying on task, if they're easily distracted).

If kids are using a desktop, laptop or a tablet for their homework (or for playing computer games, for that matter), it's wise to have them do so in a communal space where you can keep a discreet but watchful eye on what they're doing. That way, you can ensure that they're staying safe online, and also support them in learning to do that for themselves independently. Don't forget to also activate any available parental controls on your home broadband connection, including smartphones and games consoles.

The kitchen or dining room table is always a reliable option for a homework zone, but a suitably-sized desk in a corner of your kitchen or living space could do just as well – it depends on your daily routine, and where you'll ordinarily be at the time your child is doing their homework. For many people, this is in the kitchen preparing an evening meal. Other kids will enjoy doing their homework in their parents' workspace, perhaps even alongside parents who work from home and are getting on with their own tasks.

SAFE AND SECURE A desk with integrated bookshelves is a great choice – especially if your home has plasterboard/dry wall internal walls, because wall-hung bookshelves are only really dependably stable when fixed onto solid walls (above left).

TAKE INSPIRATION

Pale, neutral colour schemes (or shades of turquoise or duck egg – see opposite below left) are a good foil for the bright colours of kids' artwork, so are a great choice for their creative spaces.

IN EASY REACH Make it easy for your child to focus by keeping necessary stationery and other essentials within easy reach – and if every little thing has its own place, then you're making it easier for them to tidy up after themselves, too. Pots, tins and pencil holders can sit on the desk, but don't forget about wall-hung organizers, as these also have the benefit of keeping the work surface as clear as possible (this page).

KEEP ON DISPLAY!
Pinboards are great, but thanks to improved paint and adhesive formulas, sticking things directly to the wall needn't be a no-no any more.

SURFACE SAVVY Choose easy-clean surfaces for practicality's sake. Wipe-clean paint, low-maintenance furniture and hard flooring (also best for chairs with casters) will help you keep a work area looking its best without putting in too much time and effort. It's also a good idea to keep surfaces relatively clear, so that you don't have to embark on 'mission tidy-up' every time you want to do a quick bit of dusting (above left and right).

Older children, with more challenging and time-consuming homework tasks and greater maturity, may favour a more private space for study – many teens prefer to do so in their bedrooms, but make sure they also have the option of using a shared space if they like. Teen bedrooms can be full of distractions – drum kit, speakers, guitars, magazines – and sometimes working in a different space can be more productive.

Some kids find it easiest to focus in a calming ambience, whereas others may prefer to get in the flow on the floor in the midst of chaos and with music playing. Others like to settle down and spread out over the kitchen table, to be close to the action (and the refrigerator). Whatever their preference, if older children are allowed to choose for themselves, they're more likely to take responsibility for the standard and timeliness of their work.

For this reason, make sure you involve them in the process of choosing the elements of their workspace, so that it meshes with their preferred way of working – although there's nothing wrong with a little guidance on the practicalities of suitable furniture and storage. You'll certainly need somewhere to stash all the usual equipment, such as paper, pens, hole punches and all the rest of the homework paraphernalia.

CREATING A DEDICATED HOBBY SPACE

» If you or other family members are into sewing, needlepoint, crafting, drawing or painting, you'll not only find that a dedicated workstation can make that hobby more relaxing and enjoyable, but easy access to the necessary materials (and somewhere to safely leave that half-finished masterpiece) will mean you're more likely to find time to engage in it.

» If yours is a potentially messy hobby that involves clay, paint or other substances that can stain fabrics and unsealed materials, take this into account when you choose a work surface. That said, you don't necessarily need to choose your furniture with this in mind, as you could protect a desk or tabletop with vinyl or oilcloth, or even a sheet of toughened glass or Perspex cut for the purpose.

» As ever, good storage is imperative, and it will be easier to be creative in the space if supplies are easy to access (no cramming too many things into storage boxes and piling them on top of each other). Shelves above the work area are a good place to start, but if you don't have the wall space (or don't like the look of open shelving), a mobile trolley (find them at IKEA or hardware stores) can be wheeled out alongside you as you work, then tucked away under a desk or work surface when not in use.

Glass or metal jars, boxes or card files work well for holding smaller items such as pens, pencils or crafting materials, as do mini desktop drawers, pots and tins, with like items grouped together and ordered by colour, size or whatever else is relevant.

» Pinboards are a key element of a hobby or art and crafting space. You can pin fabric samples, tear sheets and other essentials there, to inspire creativity or simply to express your personality. And good lighting is essential for a hobby space. Add directable task lights for any close work. If your working area is small, clip-on lights can offer illumination without taking up valuable desk space.

A PLACE FOR EVERYTHING Many hobbies require a lot of supplies and equipment – and for indulging in your interest to be enjoyable, you need to keep everything in order and easily to hand, or you'll spend more time looking for things than making progress! Storage solutions such as banks of small drawers and boxes and chests of various kinds (opposite, below and below left) will ensure order and enable you to focus on the fun. Wall-hung storage systems such as pegboards (left) are particularly useful, as they can be tailored to your needs.

ORGANIZING

Nobody wants to devote much time to keeping track of a bulging pile of household bills or other correspondence, but do consider this task when planning your home. A designated area for keeping a 'to-do' pile of post or paperwork (the domestic version of an in-tray) will help prevent the kitchen counter or hall table from becoming a dumping ground, and should also alert you to the fact that there's a build-up of tasks that needs addressing.

If you're keeping on top of bill-paying, diary duties and correspondence, you may want to whizz through tasks at the kitchen table. Perhaps there's a general desk space in your living area that's shared by adults and children doing homework? Alternatively, you may decide to devote a corner to a more formal office set-up with a filing cabinet plus desktop computer.

Other good ideas for streamlining the essential elements and routines of daily life include allocating a specific area for unopened mail (or letters and parcels awaiting a trip to the post office). It's also a good idea to have a table, tray or even a drawer to hold your keys, phones and wallets (so that you are less likely to forget critical items when you are dashing out of the door in a hurry) and to hang a wall planner or calendar somewhere that the whole household can see and take heed of – no more excuses necessary for missed rubbish collections or forgotten birthdays!

Last but not least, a charging station for electronic devices prevents those annoying moments when you realize that someone has 'borrowed' your phone charger or you're about to leave home only to realize that your laptop is down to 5% battery power.

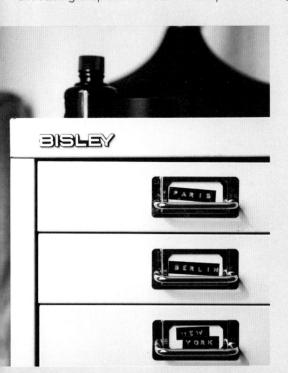

STREAMLINED STORAGE

Keeping everything in its place will make any home office or study zone easier to work in. The good news is there are plenty of innovative and easily available storage solutions out there, and a bunch of simple, affordable ones, too.

To optimize wall space, measure belongings and books and hang shelves so that there's only just adequate clearance between each one. Taking wall shelves all the way up to the ceiling will give you maximum storage capacity and stretching them across the wall also helps the cause. Documents and papers can be stored in boxes or magazine files, which look orderly when lined up on shelves. You could even paint them the same colour as the walls for a streamlined effect.

If your home office is located in a room with another function, you might decide to opt for enclosed storage so that you can put work away

at the end of the day. There are plenty of filing cabinets available nowadays that look like an attractive piece of furniture. If you can't squeeze in a filing cabinet, file paperwork in storage boxes on top of the desk or on shelves.

Small-scale storage is a must. Use lidded boxes to keep a myriad of items tidy (matching ones will create a coherent look, but an eclectic mixture can also be very appealing), and choose pegboards or other wall-hung storage systems to maximize the storage potential of the immediate desk area and help keep stationery supplies close at hand.

If you want storage to stay streamlined, have regular clear-outs and shred your old paperwork. Alternatively, you could go paperless. Invest in a desktop scanner and send scans of important documents or correspondence to your online storage system of choice.

JUST IMAGINE Vintage office furniture can strike the right note in a home study (opposite left) while repurposing objects as storage helps makes the space feel more 'home' rather than 'office'. Try mugs and tins as pen holders, picture ledges as shallow shelves above a desk or a small dining table as a desk (opposite right).

PUT IT AWAY!
A bank of matching storage boxes like this one is an inexpensive and space-saving solution. Buy more boxes than you need, in case your requirements expand.

MODULAR STORAGE SYSTEMS

When it comes to equipping a study (or living) area with adequate storage, a modular shelving system is an excellent choice. Many of them are fixed to the wall, so free up floor space, and consist of shelves, cabinets and even desktops that can be arranged (and even reorganized) as desired. Others are more akin to building blocks that can be arranged to create almost endless configurations of shelves, chests and more.

Sleek, versatile and practical, modular systems allow you to create a tailored storage solution that can be adapted to fit both the available space – even if it's cramped or awkward – and what you need to store or put on display.

In addition, modular systems are often more affordable than custom-built bookshelves and storage (although this is not always the case, so it is worth speaking to a local carpenter as well). They can also be dismantled after they've been put together, so that they can be reconfigured as your needs change or even taken with you when you move house, for maximum investment value (and sustainability creds). There are classic mid-century designs such as the USM Haller system and the Vitsoe 606 Universal Shelving System, but look at IKEA, too, as it offers several very cost-effective options.

WHERE SIZE MATTERS Whether they're supported by freestanding frameworks (affixed to the wall just to stop them toppling over), or attached to wall-hung uprights with brackets, modular storage systems are perfect for squeezing maximum functionality out of a minimal footprint. Stretching one of these systems the full height and width of a room is not only a good choice practically but often also offers the sleekest and most balanced aesthetic, too (above and opposite).

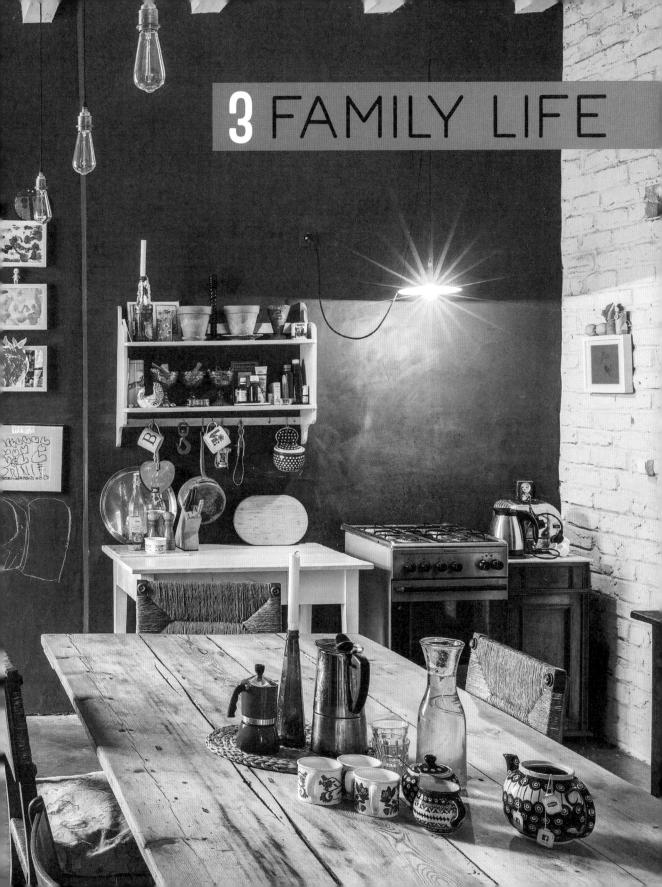

3 FAMILY LIFE

CONNECTING

When children arrive on the scene, life tends to get turned upside down for a while - not only do you have to adjust to keeping a tiny human alive while suffering from sleep deprivation, but you may also find that your home doesn't function quite as well for you as it previously did. The advent of kids is likely to mean that your living areas have to work harder than ever before - by day a toddler's playroom, by evening a home office or entertaining space. And as children grow up and their needs change, the family home has to flex, adapt and grow with them. For both parents and children, there are huge benefits to a home where everyone can gather together to eat, play, entertain and relax.

When it comes to adapting to suit a growing family, the approach is to consider how your home and furnishings can best work for you now, while keeping your mind on the future. It's all very well planning an adorable toddler's bedroom with murals of cute characters and

a pre-schooler-sized built-in bed, but in a year or two you can be sure they'll have grown out of it and be demanding a 'grown-up' bed plus enough space for their rapidly expanding Lego collection.

It's also important to think about how your home can support the building of close family ties, and enable you to spend leisure time all together. This will help kids thrive and learn good habits for later life, and also results in a less stressful day-to-day routine. Speaking of which, decor and layout choices can help in another way, too - get them right and you should be able to cut down on time spent cleaning, without having to compromise your standards of cleanliness!

EATING TOGETHER

It's no secret that family mealtimes have tremendous value – it's a time to catch up and check in with loved ones, build better family relationships and set kids on the right path when it comes to healthy eating and good table manners, as well as general social skills. If you can squeeze one in, an area where the whole family can sit down together to eat is a really, really good idea.

Whether it's in the kitchen or the living area, a proper dining table is a must. If space is an issue, look at round pedestal tables that take up less space and can be positioned in a corner. Alternatively, search for a slimline extendable table with extra wings that can be folded down when not in use (but maximized for a full family gathering) – they are available in all sorts of styles and sizes, and to suit all budgets. Make sure your dining chairs are comfy, so that you don't have fidgeting kids rushing to finish and scramble down from the table (if you have young children, highchairs that can grow with them are a great idea). Stackable chair designs can be a flexible choice, as can stackable stools for when you have unexpected visitors at mealtimes. In a small room, a bench can seat several people and be pushed away beneath the table when meals are done.

An easy-care washable hard floor is the most practical option – even more so if some family members haven't quite mastered the use of cutlery/flatware yet – and you'll certainly want to think about ease of cleaning when it comes to choosing chairs and a table, too.

HARLEQUIN SET There's no rule that says your dining chairs have to match – in fact, an eclectic selection can make for a much more interesting aesthetic (this page). It also means that everybody in the family, old and young, can have a chair that suits them best in terms of height and comfort.

EASY CHOICES Avoid fabric-upholstered chairs if you have kids – wood or even leather, like the ones shown here, are easier to clean – and a wipe-clean tabletop will save you fretting about spills when you're meant to be enjoying a family meal. A wipeable tablecloth is also a good option.

OPEN TO IDEAS The popularity of knocking through reception rooms isn't just that open plan helps smaller homes appear more spacious, it's that it enables togetherness. In this sort of space, all manner of tabletop activities (homework, art and craft, games) can take place while other family members are reading, chatting or watching TV.

HANGING OUT

Creating a living space for parents and children to share is key to a harmonious and smooth-running daily life. Such a living room offers somewhere that family members can spend time both together and apart, but devising a space that meets everyone's needs, whatever their age or life stage, can be a tricky brief.

First of all, decide on decor that suits both parties. Too kiddie, and the room won't work well for adult entertaining. Too adult, and you'll be worrying about keeping sticky fingers off the curtains. The best advice is to play it safe. Keep the walls and window treatments neutral to offset the sea of primary-coloured toys, and introduce bold colours or punchy designs in the form of upholstery, rugs and art. When you're planning the space, max out on storage – you will use it all and you won't regret it!

Choose flooring for a family sitting room wisely. If you yearn for the comfort factor of carpet yet anticipate a daily onslaught of spillages, modelling clay and crayons, it's sensible to opt for hard flooring and cover it with inexpensive rugs. These can be upgraded (or you could even opt to have the whole room carpeted) once your children are teenagers and spend every waking (and non-waking) hour lurking in their bedrooms.

Think about where you place the TV set. Make sure that chairs and sofas are positioned so that occupants can see the screen without craning or twisting their body or neck. If you've got a family-sized or modular L-shaped sofa, this can be quite simple, but if not, and the extra seating can't

TAKE INSPIRATION
Why not create some artwork as a family? Simple, abstract pictures are easy and inexpensive to create, and it's a great way for kids to feel involved and proud of their contribution to the family spaces.

THE RIGHT ANGLE Big corner sofas are just the ticket for the whole family to pile onto, whether they're playing a board game, watching a film, or just having a quiet read or a cosy cuddle (left). Choose something with maximum squish for comfort, or at the very least pile it high with comfy cushions and a throw (or two, or three...) for snuggling up in cosily.

be easily repositioned (in small rooms you may not have quite as much flexibility), then a couple of squishy beanbags or pouffes will be a savvy addition to your space. You can dial up the comfort factor with extra cushions and a snug throw or two for cosying up, as well as a couple of side tables (or even low stools) to keep drinks and snacks within immediate reach. A large coffee table provides an ideal surface for playing, drawing and snacking – again, think about practicality. If you have young children, this may not be the time to choose a valuable antique.

TV sets seem to be getting larger and larger by the year. A big black screen can be quite a dominant presence in a room, so if that doesn't appeal, or if you're keen on a home cinema set-up, then consider fitting a projector and screen. Attaching the projector to your ceiling is a specialized task, but once it's done, the viewing experience is akin to a trip to the movie theatre. You'll need to consider lighting carefully if you want to achieve that authentic cinema ambience. Make sure the light levels in your room are dimmable – either with adjustable switches or through simply turning the main wall or ceiling lights off and a couple of side lamps on – and also that there's no reflective glow on the screen caused by a badly placed light fitting.

LET THERE BE LIGHT Creating the right ambience while balancing practical need for light is even more important in a multifunctional space. Bright rooms are pleasant to be in, but if you want to enjoy a family film on a sunny Sunday morning, you'll be able to choose cinema-style darkness if you hang some heavy curtains or fit blackout blinds. It's also important to ensure that plenty of thought is given to task lighting – nobody wants to be squinting at a book, or working in their own shadow when indulging in creative hobbies. Table and standard lamps are good, flexible choices to fulfil this need.

FITTING A BABY INTO YOUR BEDROOM

» Based on numerous studies from around the world, experts advise that newborns should sleep in their parents' room (but not their bed) for the first six months of their lives to reduce the risk of SIDS. If your bedroom space is already at a premium, this can demand some reorganization.

» You'll want your baby to sleep as close to you as possible (it makes things that much easier when you're waking in the night), so try to figure out the best way to do this - even if you have to temporarily change the layout of your room to do so. Moses baskets/bassinets on a folding stand are a good choice where space is tight, but after a few months it will be time to transfer junior to a cot/crib. A bedside/side-sleeping cot/crib that attaches to your bed so that you can easily lift baby out for night-time feeds is a popular option and allows your baby to safely sleep alongside his or her parents.

» If you have space for a cot/crib, then a cot/crib-top changer is a great space-saver - although a changing mat on the floor does the job perfectly well (and there's zero chance of your child falling if they roll over). A nursing chair can also be a handy addition, but only if the room can accommodate one that's comfy (otherwise you probably won't actually use it).

» It's also a good idea to pay some extra attention to routes around the room, since you'll be moving around the space only half-awake sometimes, and you may have a newborn in your arms when you do so. Make sure that you remove all trip hazards, and try to maximize the space available for manoeuvring so that there's less risk of colliding with a door or walking into the corner of a piece of furniture.

SAFETY FIRST There's something beautiful about vintage or antique cots/cribs - but if you're thinking about using one, make sure you evaluate it carefully for safety using modern guidelines (above).

TIME FLIES Many modest homes (especially new-builds) have bedrooms that are only just big enough for a bed and minimal storage furniture (indeed, in some places, especially city dwellings, there's only just space for the bed!). If this scenario sounds familiar, and squeezing in even a Moses basket/bassinet is tricky and makes the room seem cluttered and awkward, remember that the newborn stage is over remarkably rapidly, and your child will soon be in their own room – they grow up far too quickly!

PLAYING

The most likely candidate for a dual-purpose space that includes a play area is going to be the living room - after all, play is 'living' for the younger members of the family, and it's healthy to foster a relaxed, inclusive atmosphere. In addition, living rooms are often the largest spaces in an apartment or house, so there tends to be more space to accommodate a play zone. But there are many other options. Hallways and landings are ideal for spreading out and setting up train sets, racing toy cars or skipping and hopscotch. If you have a spare

corner in the kitchen, a mini workbench or oven will keep toddlers happy for hours. Children learn from creative and imaginary play and love to make dens and create 'camps', so in the sitting room a pop-up playhouse or tipi offers somewhere for play, naps and reading. A large sheet thrown over the dining room table can create a hidey hole where kids will hang out for hours. Space is always at a premium in a family home, but even the smallest nooks and crannies can offer an inspiring play environment.

As children grow and change, so do their notions of play. While hanging out in front of a favourite movie is a great way to spend family time, why not switch things up with board games, cards or jigsaws? Not only are such activities a more interactive experience than watching TV, but your kids can also practise important life skills: turn-taking, patience, strategy, focus, problem-solving, communication, creativity… You'll need a surface big enough for whatever game you're playing and comfy seats for everyone. If your coffee table isn't big enough, you could always put a board on top to extend its area.

LIVING ROOM PLAY AREAS

The biggest impact that adding a play area will have on your living room is likely to be in layout considerations – the bigger the floor area you can make available for play, the better. If your space is long and narrow, then a dedicated play zone tucked away at one end might be the best choice, but if the room is compact and square-ish, then you'll probably want to keep the centre of the room as clear as you can. Depending on the configuration of your space, you may be able to carve out space for a play area by positioning the sofa so that it becomes a divider, giving little ones a neatly delineated place that's their territory.

The easiest way to instantly demarcate a play area is with a rug (opt for something sturdy that will withstand stains and spills), which will also provide a soft surface to crawl or sit on. If at all possible, site toy storage nearby for ease of tidying up at the end of the day. Try tucking a storage bench or low-level unit close to the play zone. If that's really not possible, the next-best solution is to make provision elsewhere, and ensure that kids have a way of easily carrying toys to their play area (and back again) – perhaps a storage box with handles or wheels on, or a basket (they'd probably be even more keen to get involved if you popped their name on it, too). Awkward or unused nooks or corners can be transformed into a cosy reading area – dress with a couple of beanbags that can be put away when you're entertaining and perhaps even hang a book rack on the wall.

Great seating is absolutely key for all living rooms, so make sure you get your sofa right. Find the biggest one possible for the space you have available, so that you can all cuddle up together to watch TV. Choosing one that has robust upholstery in a darkish colour or pattern is essential, as small kids are bound to scramble all over it, and sticky hands and juice spillages are always a risk. L-shaped modular seating is an excllent choice – it can double up as a bed for sleepovers or even adult guests. Add a couple of armchairs and a pouffe or beanbag and you're done.

If possible, a mini table plus chairs is a great addition – tuck them into a corner or beneath the window for puzzles, Lego sessions and reading. The living room may not be the natural home for art and crafting activities or indeed anything that involves paint or glue – see page 120 for suggestions for containing messy play.

THINK SMALL Adding pint-sized furniture to your living room will not only delight young children but create a clear 'play zone' that's ideal for drawing, toys and play (above).

TAKE INSPIRATION

White walls can help ensure
that a space filled with brightly
coloured toys and books
doesn't feel overwhelming –
while mixing in the natural
textures of wood adds
a more mature, tactile
edge to the aesthetic.

KEEP ON DISPLAY! Everything from art supplies to board game boxes can make for a colourful and attractive display (especially against a white backdrop), so don't feel you have to hide everything away.

TOY AND GAMES STORAGE

CONTAIN YOURSELF There's no need to stick to purpose-made boxes and chests – with a bit of imagination, anything can be pressed into use as toy storage. Here (opposite below) a sewing box has been used to create a toddler-height library, watched over by a couple of soft toys given a home in its pouch.

The key to winning at toy and game storage is to keep everything low level – child-height solutions mean that kids are able to choose what they'd like to play with for themselves and, crucially, can tidy away without help (well, perhaps not entirely alone – they will need a reminder or two, of course!). Low-level storage units can be kitted out with boxes and baskets for fast tidying. Under-bed or under-sofa storage is also a winner. Simply pull out storage boxes or carts on wheels, throw everything in and push away out of sight. Shallow boxes make items easy to spot and easily accessible for little ones. Storage benches are also ideal for quick

tidying sessions. You can try to make tidying less painful by setting an oven timer for three minutes and telling everyone to do as much as they can in the time allowed – this introduces a competitive element that often appeals to small children!

Another secret to success is to provide storage that allows for separating different toys, so all the building blocks are together, all the doll's clothes, all the dress-up clothes and so on. Sure, these neat groupings might not be stuck to (and it's better to turn a blind eye to this than put a child off tidying up altogether), but at least it's possible to keep some kind of order, and start nurturing good

organizational habits. Get a large bin (or laundry bag) so that you can fling in all those bulky stuffed animals and push it into a corner or behind a sofa. If at all possible, have picture books out on a child-height bookshelf or display unit, but if that doesn't work, stack them in crates or a magazine rack instead.

Bear in mind that not all the toys need to be accessible all the time. Having fewer items on offer and rotating toys every week or couple of weeks means that kids won't get bored with their possessions and there won't be as many toys to wrangle at the end of the day. A double win! Another way to keep on top of toy storage is to have regular decluttering sessions. Any broken toys or games with lost pieces can go, as can toys that your children have outgrown – share with neighbours or take them to the charity/thrift store.

EASY DOES IT Make it simple for young kids to tidy up independently, and rotate available toys routinely to make sure the collection doesn't outgrow storage capacity – little ones will be delighted to find 'new' toys at regular intervals (this page)!

RECLAIMING GROWN-UP SPACE

» As a bit of grown-up time is essential for parental sanity, it's important to make sure you have a way of converting your living room back into a relaxing adult haven at the end of the day. Good toy storage will facilitate this, especially if it completely (or even just mostly) hides all your child's brightly coloured paraphernalia and looks good when the toys are stashed away.

» A flat-topped toy chest (in a colour that suits your decor) can function as a coffee table after bedtime (as well as a handy surface for board games or construction toys during playtime). Under-bed boxes that roll underneath your sofas are a good addition to hold overflow bits and pieces. Alternatively, you could hide the toy-storage zone behind a sofa, a curtain or a folding screen. If you have a pop-up playhouse, put boxes, baskets and other items inside. OK, you may have a miniature pink palace in one corner of the living room, but at least all the other junk is hidden away out of sight.

» The other way to flip the atmosphere to a more serene adult one is to use lighting - position a number of lamps or lanterns around the room, and simply by turning them on and turning off the main pendants, you can create a cosier, more sophisticated feel.

» You might also want to choose play-area elements that can be whipped away and stored out of sight. Stackable chairs and tables can work well (though do make sure you choose child-safe designs), while a play mat or brightly coloured rug can be rolled up and pushed under or behind the sofa. On the subject of the sofa, you may want to fling a child-friendly throw over it during the day to protect it from crayons, juice spills and sticky fingers. After bedtime, whip it off and fold it up for the evening.

HIDDEN TREASURE Integrating toy storage into furniture - then concealing it - is a great tactic for making sure you can reclaim your room at the end of the day. The sofa above (made from storage boxes with casters) can simply be covered with a throw.

LIVING IN HARMONY In this Danish home, the light-flooded double-height sitting room is a space shared by adults and children. The colourful playhouse is perfect for imaginative play, yet easy to take down at the end of the day (or to use as storage for other toys).

YOUNG ARTISTS AND MESSY PLAY

Letting your child make art or indulge in wet or messy play indoors isn't for the faint-hearted, especially if your home is small. There are plenty of people who choose to do this sort of activity outside or at playgroups or art and craft sessions, which is a perfectly valid choice. However, with some pre-planning you can make it easy to tidy up (and lower the risk of ruining the flooring or furnishings) and give your child an opportunity to play and learn creatively at home.

The best spots for these activities are usually the kitchen or dining area, because surfaces are often wipe-clean and stain-resistant. It's worth covering up the floor and table anyway just in case, and to make clean-up easier. Invest in a heavy-duty splash mat or messy mat to go underneath the table while your kids get in touch with their inner Picasso. Alternatively, you could buy an inexpensive fold-up table or a child's easel specifically for crafty moments and pop these on a splash mat to protect the floor. If kids are using modelling materials, cover the tabletop with vinyl or oilcloth, then encourage them to work in a large shallow tray to contain the mess.

One of the best choices you can make in any family home is to decorate with tough, scrubbable paint on the walls. Get the right formula, and you will be amazed what can be cleaned off (although choice of artist's materials also has a bearing here; look for washable water-based paints and pens for younger children – no Sharpies or acrylics!).

If the thought of face paint smeared all over the sofa makes you anxious, the bathtub can be a great spot for messy play and it's easy to clean up, too – just hose everything down with a hand-held shower afterwards.

PUT IT AWAY!
Keep art materials in their proper place – but not just because you're being neat and tidy (opposite). You'll also guard against wall doodles caused by tempting pens and paints left out within reach!

TOP CHOICE A big, robust dining table is the ideal place for youngsters to paint, draw and model – and if it's situated in an open-plan space with hard-wearing, wipeable surfaces, then so much the better (this page). In this kitchen-diner, busy parents can combine meal prep, or other essential tasks such as laundry, with keeping an eye on their kids' creative endeavours.

Children love to create and, equally, love to see their masterpieces displayed in their home. But there's a fine balance between celebrating your children's artistic talents and their artworks taking over the space so that it ends up looking like a classroom. Luckily, there are all sorts of ways to exhibit kids' art in your home without allowing it to dominate.

Invest in a large corkboard, or identify one wall or the back of a door and use it to display an ever-changing gallery of masterpieces. This approach works well in a kitchen area, which tends to have a more informal family vibe. Artworks can also look very effective hung on a large pinboard over a desk or other workstation, where you can mix in postcards, tear sheets and photos. Kids may like to have a small pinboard each, where they can curate drawings, photos and other clippings.

Another fun way of hanging pictures is from a long washing line with decorative wooden pegs. The pictures can easily be changed and make a nice change from strings of bunting or fairy lights. Make sure any string is secured to the walls high up and well out of the way of little children.

Chalkboard paint is your friend when it comes to encouraging creativity and a quiet pastime for kids to engage in. Whether you choose to paint a board, a door or even a wall with the paint, it gives children a place where they can give free rein to their imagination and scribble away on a large surface to their hearts' content. It also provides adults

DISPLAYING CHILDREN'S CREATIONS

with a handy spot to jot down shopping lists and other household reminders. And you don't have to worry about hanging artworks, as the chalkboard acts as a blank canvas for your kids' creations. A chalkboard wall is also a great idea for a teen bedroom, allowing a creative youngster to graffiti all over it without causing permanent marks. It's a boon that dark walls can look very effective decoratively speaking, especially when set against wooden furniture and floors.

If you're living in rented property, you may not have the luxury of painting the walls with chalkboard paint (or anything else, for that matter). If this is the case, stick up artworks, postcards and photos using washi tape, which will peel off walls without leaving a mark. Command strips are a brilliant solution if you aren't able to stick up pictures or hammer a nail in the wall – they won't damage paintwork as long as they're removed carefully according to the instructions.

PICK AND MIX It's easy to find yourself drowning in artwork brought back from school or created at home, but with a little forethought you can curate an interior-enhancing display of unique images (below and opposite). Get your kids involved in choosing their favourite masterpieces; they'll not only feel more important and their opinions valued, but they might just develop a more discerning eye for a picture, too.

FLOORING FOR
SHARED SPACES

» Household flooring takes a fierce pounding every day, so deserves careful consideration. If you're lucky enough to have space for a separate playroom, then the choice is easy - practicality dictates that washable is the way to go, so laminate, rubber or vinyl are obvious options. The last two tend to be warmer and softer underfoot, with or without rugs on top to create a more comfortable spot for little bottoms to sit on.

» However, in a space that has to do double duty as a dining or living room (or any other room for that matter), you probably don't want nursery-style flooring having a significant impact on your decorative choices. Laminate is still a valid choice here, but well-sealed solid or engineered wooden flooring offers similar practicality with a more luxurious appearance. If you're on a tight budget, sanding and varnishing or painting any existing floorboards could be a good option (though do make sure to fill any gaps between boards as part of the process, to avoid chilly draughts). Wood is an excellent option for high-traffic areas, and a quick sweep and vacuum plus a weekly mopping will keep it clean.

» Rugs not only soften an interior (and improve the acoustics) but also help to visually zone a shared space. You could position one under the dining table to demarcate that as a different area to the seating area - an adult domain or a place for entertaining, for example. For a play area, look for a rug that will soften the surface for toddlers or crawlers - a synthetic fibre rug will be the most resistant to spills, stains and everyday wear.

» For the littlest littlies, it's worth investing in a big play mat, too - nothing fancy required, either a quilt-style fabric version, or the interlocking foam tile type (pictured below). Whatever you choose, make sure you think about small feet and trip hazards - use non-slip pads or anti-slip underlay beneath rugs.

FEELING GROUNDED Spills are a given when you have small children, so an easily washable hard flooring, like the examples shown on this page, is a bit of a no-brainer. Younger kids spend a lot of time in close contact with the floor, so as well as being practical, the surface has to be comfortable (washable rugs in strategic places are a good option). Hard floors can feel cold underfoot (especially stone and tile), so it could be well worth having electric underfloor heating installed to take the edge off.

4 MAKE MORE SPACE

UNLOVED SPACES

When it comes to improving the functionality of your home, it's surprising how much positive impact can be achieved by taking a close look at where you might carve out extra space. Look for nooks, corners and even walls that don't see much use but have potential for either storage or a specific activity.

Take a wander around your home, focusing on the underused areas. Once you've identified fallow space, the next step is to figure out what it could be used for. Location is important. A study space carved out of a spare corner is likely to be less successful if it's close to the TV, or abuts a party wall with noisy neighbours on the other side. Be realistic. There's no point in spending time crafting a reading nook if you've not picked up a book in the past year, or deciding that an alcove in the hallway would be perfect for displaying glassware when the fact that you'd have to carry fragile objects through the house each time you want to use them makes the idea impractical.

Thinking outside the box reaps rewards. A niche between two wardrobes might be wide enough for a wall-hung desktop, giving an awkward space an identity. In the living room, the gap beneath a loose-covered/slipcovered sofa/couch is ideal for storing flat items such as folding chairs (or anything else, for that matter - a cover with a floor-length skirt is effective at hiding all manner of objects).

When it comes to storage, if an object fits, and you're not putting something that's used daily in a hard-to-reach place, it's worth considering as a solution. And when it comes to creating a spot for a specific activity, the practical considerations are, quite simply, will it fit, and will it work for you?

UNDER THE STAIRS

Unless your home is all on a single level, a prime candidate for carving out extra space is underneath the staircase – the restricted head height here and often in a hallway location may seem to be a limiting factor, but there are actually many different uses for this area.

The most obvious of these is storage. Many homes already have hooks, racks and shelving for shoes and outerwear in this location, but custom-built fitted solutions (which don't have to be expensive) offer maximum use of space and, when designed with pull-out functionality, maximum accessibility, too. Made-to-measure shelving could also transform this area into a library space or even a display area for a collection. But storage and display are not the only options by any stretch of the imagination.

Pop a low-slung comfy armchair under the least-head-height-restricted side, and a low sideboard/credenza or shelves at the most-restricted side, and you have the perfect spot to curl up with a book. Find a compact desk and a chair that slides unobtrusively beneath it, and you have an office nook that's a handy spot for carrying out all the household admin. If you have a dog, consider whether this might be the best place for their bed – or if you are a cat owner, you could think about concealing the litter tray in an understairs cupboard. This is also a good spot to hold those less than glamorous but nonetheless essential recycling facilities.

Depending on the limitations of the space, you could choose something a little less ordinary for the understairs area. Cramped kitchen and no utility area? Install laundry appliances (and maybe a drying rack) under the stairs behind large cupboard doors. Only have one WC? Look into

whether it's possible to fit a compact cloakroom into this space. Entertain a lot, and have a staircase rising from your living or dining area? Consider an on-trend wet bar, or even just a drinks-making station and wine rack if you don't fancy shelling out for plumbing works.

Other options might also be worth giving thought to, if they suit your circumstances. In a tiny house, you could squeeze a kitchenette in under the stairs, or a wine enthusiast might build a custom wine rack (since the location is often appropriately lacking in direct sunlight and temperature fluctuations), while in an open-plan layout, the understairs area might be a natural choice for a kids' play area (or for toy storage).

OUT OF SIGHT Being able to literally close the door on work, and hide your home office away behind cupboard doors, is a great way to support work/life balance (above).

STORAGE TETRIS This basement study-studio uses every inch of space to its full potential – the chest of drawers has been placed as far as it will go under the stairs, and to its left you can see the storage boxes that give even this awkward corner a useful purpose.

MODERN MINIMALIST If your home is modest in size, then it can be a savvy move to make your understairs solution really sleek and minimalist, with clutter hidden away. Handle-free sprung push-catch doors offer the most streamlined way to access the storage space that can be squeezed in under the stairs – many smaller homes are crying out for such a capacious cupboard (left).

KEEP ON DISPLAY!
Under the stairs isn't ideal for display – turning your shelves at right angles instead can work better. A cosy reading nook makes better use of the space.

DEEP DIVE Consider the depth of your stairs when you're thinking about how best to use the understairs space. If you're planning to use this area for storage, then you'll need to plan it in such a way that you can easily reach all the way to the back. You could use boxes or baskets that can be dragged out when you want to access their contents, or maybe opt for a built-in solution with pull-out drawers or sections that can be moved about on casters (left). A deep staircase may offer the option of a cloakroom (below left) while a shallower flight is easier to work around (below).

HALLWAYS AND LANDINGS

Usually in a quieter location – upstairs, where there is perhaps less through traffic – hallways and landings lend themselves to more meditative activities, or those that require greater focus. For this reason, they are ideally situated for a home office or reading nook – even more so than under the stairs, both because of the relative quiet and the chances of them offering up a larger area (depending on the layout of your home).

These characteristics also give the landing a broader scope when it comes to the possibilities. If you can fit in a narrow console table that's just wide enough to accommodate a laptop and a small lamp, you've got an instant work zone. Keep a folding chair tucked behind the bedroom door so that it doesn't clutter the space. A wide upstairs hallway might allow for a single sofa bed, providing extra guest capacity (though admittedly only for the sort of guest comfortable with the level of privacy a hallway affords!).

Could you fit in some freestanding storage – maybe there's enough room for a linen press, bookshelves or a sideboard/credenza? Beneath a window is the spot for a built-in window seat-cum-storage bench. If the space is sizeable enough, you might even be able to fit in a freestanding love seat or compact two-seater sofa/couch with a slim reading lamp to create an additional seating area. Wide staircases and hallways are also a great spot to locate a run of custom-built bookshelves, as are half-landings on a staircase.

If there isn't floor space for any furniture, look at the walls. If you have a large expanse of empty wall, could this be a spot for a gallery wall-type hanging, a collection of family photographs or even two or three picture shelves where you can prop up artworks to create a mini gallery area? A narrow hallway will also be brightened up by the addition of a large wall mirror.

TAKE INSPIRATION
A wide, shallow space at the top of a staircase is the perfect spot for a slimline seat (left). Antique and vintage models often have a narrower profile than their modern counterparts.

THINK LATERALLY Even a small return on a landing can offer a variety of functions, but it is a particularly useful spot for the home office, which often doesn't need a huge footprint (right and above right). If the fallow space at the end of the landing doesn't quite offer sufficient room for a suitable desk, it's worth considering whether a small tweak to the floor's layout might be in order – moving a doorway a few feet in one direction may make all the difference.

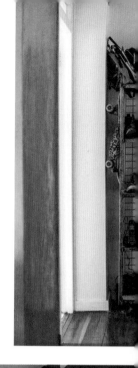

EVERY LITTLE COUNTS Look for opportunities for extra storage on a hallway or landing. Even a narrow corridor can accommodate a coat hook or two, and as long as there's space to walk past without difficulty, you can put an appropriately sized piece of storage in a spare corner or place narrow shelving along the walls. Where space is tight, it's particularly important to source furniture that fits comfortably (this page).

MORE PLEASE Don't make the mistake of underestimating the amount of hallway storage you'll need, especially if you have a family. If your entryway only has room for wall-hung hooks and a few pairs of shoes, keep just seasonally appropriate clothing there, and store the out-of-season pieces in a box or wardrobe/ closet elsewhere (this page and opposite below left).

TAKE INSPIRATION
In a small or awkward space, too much going on can be overwhelming. Bear in mind that a neutral or restricted colour palette, as shown here, can help a busy area seem calmer, especially if it's likely to be home to a variety of assorted clutter.

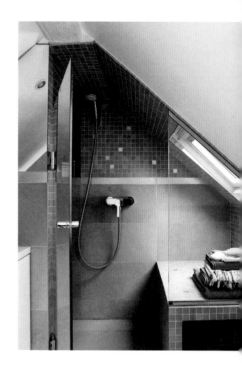

ATTICS AND LOFTS

Depending on the age and construction of your house or top-floor apartment, you may either have attic rooms or a loft, and provided that the head height isn't too restrictive, this potential additional square footage offers you the opportunity to carve out some extra space in your home. Of course, it will cost more to make such spaces properly habitable; remember that any major works should always be carried out by a competent contractor and in accordance with building regulations.

The majority of loft conversions are undertaken to provide an extra bedroom (usually with an ensuite bathroom or shower), but that's not to say it's the only option for a roof space. If the light is good (perhaps through the addition of several skylights or dormer windows), such a space can make a quiet and secluded home office or a brilliant artist's studio or crafting space. Even

if there's not a huge amount of natural light, it could still be transformed into a useful (and beautiful) playroom, a teenage den or a guest room – basically, almost any type of room you could envisage, such is the floor space.

Loft conversions can often be architecturally awkward, with sloping ceilings, exposed beams and chimney breasts. Again, you'll have to think laterally about using those empty nooks and crannies in a way that's both practical and attractive. One of the most efficient uses of space is half-height under-eaves storage. Built-in cupboards will be the most streamlined option, but it's also possible to use a run of curtains. Tiny crawl spaces like the one in the gable of a roof can make a great hidey hole for small children. And unused alcoves can be filled with open shelving to hold books or whatever else you fancy.

LIGHTEN UP Attics and lofts can be fairly dark if there aren't many rooflights, with complex interior architecture and often rather awkward dimensions. These decorative challenges can often be countered with a pale, neutral colour scheme – featuring some natural tones and textures for contrast – which helps to simplify the complexity of the room and create a more restful space (this page and opposite).

DEALING WITH LOW CEILINGS

» Whatever the reason for the restricted head height - be it because you live in an old cottage or basement apartment, or because you have attic rooms that have been converted to living space - the same approach can be taken to make the most of the space you do have.

» Position your furniture to ensure the flow of the layout is easy; nobody wants to duck just to get from the doorway to the sofa/couch.

» Visual tricks such as floor-length curtains or internal doors that go all the way up to the ceiling are great for giving an impression of height.

» For a pared-down and restful look, keep the furniture low slung, and don't cover the wall space with shelves or busy pictures.

» Alternatively, you could go crazy with bold colour, pattern and decorative details, to create a cosy, cocoon-like space without corners or boundaries, which can trick the eye into believing a space is bigger than it really is.

» Draw the eye away from the less-than-ideal ceiling height with a bold feature wall, large mirror or statement piece of furniture.

» Increase illumination, particularly on the ceiling - use uplighters to wash light over the walls, tall lamps in dark corners and table lamps wherever possible.

» Ceiling light fittings must be flush or on short hangings - or just use lamps and wall lights for your lighting scheme. Alternatively, suspend a pendant fitting over a piece of furniture (over a bedside table/nightstand or coffee table, perhaps) so there's no danger of walking into it as you cross the room.

A HEAD FOR HEIGHTS One of the key considerations when it comes to arranging the layout of an attic or loft space is the headroom. Think carefully about how best to use the areas with restricted height so that this attribute doesn't impact on function. Popular choices include the headboard of a bed (just don't sit up suddenly in the night!), a bathing space with a low-level tub or a bespoke shower enclosure built in, or low-level storage, especially of the built-in variety (this page and opposite).

WHAT LIES BENEATH A storage bed is never not a good idea. Whether you hack one yourself from flatpack chests of drawers or have something made bespoke, a built-in that fits an awkward spot perfectly (within reason, of course – it needs to be big enough to sleep in!) can help make a very small room function as a bedroom, complete with adequate storage provision (left). For maximum cupboard space, go for a higher-level bed – a mid-sleeper or cabin-height bed doesn't have to just be the preserve of a child's room.

SOLUTIONS FOR AWKWARD SPACES

Every home has awkward corners that not only mean the space is under used but can also seem aesthetically problematic, too. One of the ways to solve these issues is with bespoke storage solutions. Built-in cupboards and shelves allow you to use the available space more efficiently, as well as giving you the opportunity to streamline or square off rooms with odd angles or balance out interiors with less-than-ideal proportions.

However, that's not to say that the tailor-made option is only to be kept for problem solving; it's amazing how much functionality can be squeezed out of a compact space when everyday fixtures and furnishings are designed to incorporate storage capacity.

A tiny utility room can be much improved with integrated appliances built into a bank of fitted units (or freestanding appliances hidden behind sliding doors or in cupboards), an otherwise purposeless alcove offers the perfect opportunity

for a fitted cupboard, while an old airing/ hot cupboard can become much more usable if you have proper shelving fitted inside. Or think even more creatively: why not construct a storage platform underneath your bed (making the room split-level) complete with trapdoor-style access to the void below; or consider hidden cupboards in panelling; even broad stairs with hinged treads that lift to reveal storage compartments.

PERFECT FIT Even the smallest corner is worth a shelf or two, while anywhere with the right volume (a bed, a sofa/couch, an alcove) is a candidate for a hiding place for life's essentials – and non-essentials (this page).

HIDE AND SEEK Storage that hides away the paraphernalia of everyday life will help to keep your home looking neat and well-ordered, and allows the emphasis to be on the decorative pieces that you choose to display. An uncluttered home looks more spacious and helps create a sense of calm, too. Whether you hide your bits and pieces in unusual places, such as these stair compartments and bookshelf headboard (left and below left), or in more standard cupboards (below), the key is to make sure things in everyday use are kept close to where they're needed. If they're not, life becomes unnecessarily inefficient.

PUT IT AWAY!
Organizing large closets and cupboards using storage boxes helps maximize both storage capacity and the ease of finding what you need when you need it.

WINDOW ON THE WORLD Window seats are a great example of carving extra functionality out of your home in a way that matches the attributes of the space. Ideal for reading or relaxing, they're light and bright (and hopefully feature an attractive view), which is always a mood-booster, plus the space underneath the seating is a prime candidate for storage provision. If you don't have the budget for a built-in like the ones shown here, but space allows, consider using a single storage bed (piled with cushions) in front of a window to achieve a similar combination of seating and storage.

5 AWAY FROM IT ALL

SLEEPING

Without a doubt, life has become more hectic than it used to be. Along with the convenience of instant communications, social media and 24/7 connectivity has come the pressure to be always 'on' and to respond immediately to every message, comment or post.

Daily life has its challenges. Commuting is stressful and tiring. On the flip side, working from home means that for many of us the boundaries between work and relaxation have become blurred and it's easy to find yourself answering emails in bed at midnight – not good for anyone's health and wellbeing. As a result, it's become more important than ever to have a space that you can retreat to, and with a little thought and some simple tweaks, it's possible to maximize your home's potential to be a nurturing space that allows its inhabitants to decompress and recharge.

Generally speaking, the rooms that work best as a retreat from the busy world are the private ones: bedrooms and bathrooms. Since they tend to be hidden away from visitors, these rooms can also be the ones that get forgotten when it comes to decorating, decluttering and tidying. But it's well worth devoting some thought to a space that can improve your wellbeing.

You may also find that you have other options for nurturing spaces. If you live alone or just with your partner, perhaps you can create a dedicated sanctuary spot in another part of your home, if there's scope for it? The end of a hallway may have the potential to be a meditation spot, or a tiny spare bedroom that's not in daily use could act as a yoga space or hobby area. Whatever you decide on, it should be a spot that facilitates relaxation or your favourite activities.

CREATING A CHILLED SLEEP SPACE

SIMPLE PLEASURES There's no need to avoid pattern or colour, but one way to ensure a calmer sleeping space is to keep the look pared down; only include elements you love, and pay particular attention to clearing visual clutter (above left and right).

When it comes to creating the ultimate bedroom relaxation zone (whether for sleeping, reading in bed or doing half an hour's yoga), think about soothing all the senses: the space needs to be warm and quiet, it needs to be comfortable and it needs to be visually calm.

If you can, locate your bedroom away from busy, noisy areas – not right next to the room where your laundry appliances are, for example, or the other side of the wall from neighbours who are addicted to late-night TV. If you can't avoid noise in this way, soundproofing can help. Lining the walls with insulation may be beyond your DIY skills or budget, but think about arranging furniture such as wardrobes along a wall to muffle the noise coming through. Soft furnishings will also absorb sound, so if you suffer from a lot of outside noise, try putting down thick rugs and hanging lined curtains as well as blinds/shades. Fabric or textile wall hangings will block noise and add a cosy vibe that's conducive to a good night's sleep.

Clutter-free rooms will automatically seem calmer, although that doesn't mean you have to opt for minimalism over your preferred style.

Simply tackling any chaos should do the trick – put away those clothes scattered on chairs or draped over the bed frame, the piles of shoes, stacks of books and so on. Sorting out suitable storage for such items is the key to a calm interior. A restricted colour palette (avoiding anything too stimulating, such as lime green or fuchsia pink) will also help your sleep space to exude a sense of tranquillity – peaceful shades of blues, greys and soft greens, along with off-whites and muted neutrals, are all calming choices.

Think carefully about what you hang on the walls. Lots of artworks can create a visual 'noise' that can be distracting. This is the spot for serene, contemplative images that aid relaxation, or textile wall hangings as mentioned opposite.

TONE ON TONE A restricted colour palette of pale neutrals makes it easy to create a calm ambience. If you're taking this approach, focus on texture to add interest – and punctuate with contrasting accents (in this case, the darker tones of natural timber and iron).

TAKE INSPIRATION
An all-white bedroom lends itself to being a gallery space. Pay attention to balance and harmony when curating your decorative displays, to ensure a sense of calm is maintained.

As well as avoiding food and drink that might keep you tossing and turning at night (such as rich, heavy dishes and coffee), and not napping too much during the day, the way your bedroom is arranged can also help promote a good night's sleep.

Think about creating an optimum night-time environment. For starters, the room should be dark (consider blackout blinds/shades especially if you live somewhere that doesn't get fully dark at night for part of the year), and the ideal temperature is 16–18 degrees Celsius/60–64 degrees Fahrenheit, so set your thermostat accordingly. The comfort levels of your bed are also imperative: choose a mattress and pillows to suit your shape and build,

as well as your sleeping position – they need to offer the right levels of support and comfort, so that you're not left feeling tired and achy when you wake.

It's also helpful if you associate your bedroom with one primary activity – sleeping. Not working out, watching TV or working on a laptop in bed. In fact, the bright light from TV screens, phones or tablets can make it difficult to fall asleep, because electronics emit a type of blue light that suppresses the production of melatonin, the hormone that makes you feel sleepy. It's best not to use these in the bedroom just before tucking yourself in for the night – preferably, avoid temptation and plan your bedroom without the addition of a TV in the first place! Some people go further and make the bedroom an electronic-free zone.

It's also a good idea to opt for lower-wattage, warm-toned bulbs so that your bedside lamp doesn't have a similar sleep-affecting consequence. And make sure your alarm clock doesn't distract you – a dazzling LED display will not only light up the room but cause stress as you watch the hours tick by.

PILLOW TALK Sumptuous headboards and ornate bedsteads certainly have their place, but for a streamlined, spartan-chic approach, choose a plain divan/boxpring bed and pile it with comfy pillows to stop your head from bumping or marking the wall (below left and right). If the bed is low level, this will also help keep the aesthetic unfussy, and emphasizes the volume of the room for a more spacious feel.

CREATING A COSY VIBE

» Whether you're renting or you've just moved into your own home but don't have the funds to decorate as you'd like, sometimes a bedroom can feel a little soulless and sterile. The good news is that there are definitely a few things you can do to up the cosiness factor, even on a tight budget.

» Most people think that bringing warm colour into a space will help it feel cosier, but this can be difficult if you're renting and bound by the terms of the contract from painting the walls. Don't be disheartened. What will have an even greater impact is adding texture. Layering a variety of contrasting surfaces and materials will bring about a tactile, homely ambience (even if you decide to keep the scheme one colour - this tactic even works to make a white-on-white interior seem welcoming). And introducing texture has the added benefit of absorbing noise and enhancing insulation - perfect for a cosy sleeping space.

» You can do this inexpensively by layering up soft furnishings, rugs, pictures and ornaments. If your budget is next to nothing, get on a local classified ad website like Craigslist or Gumtree to see what's on offer there. It's surprising what people are often selling for a song. You can also frequent charity shops/thrift stores and car boot/yard sales. If you're handy, try upcycling existing belongings (it's amazing what a spot of dye or some embroidery can do), or creating your own artworks. Framed wallpaper samples or found objects such as driftwood can add warmth, personality and cosiness to a space.

TOUCHY FEELY Think about the feel of the surfaces and materials you're using; it's not just the visual texture of a soft furnishing or a piece of furniture that makes it appealing, it's the tactile quality, too. Soft, natural fibres such as wool, cotton and linen will always trump synthetics (opposite above), while furniture made in polished natural wood or with painted surfaces that have a soft patina will look cosier than particleboard flat-pack ever could (below and opposite below).

CHOOSING
A BED

PERFECT PICK One of the most common mistakes people make is choosing a bed that's too big, or too ornate, for their space. Rather than convey a sense of sumptuous luxury, this can make a room feel cramped and awkward. As a general rule, choosing smaller, simpler designs like the ones shown here is the savvy way to go in a standard-sized bedroom – and if your chosen bed has storage integrated into the base, then so much the better (opposite above). It's amazing how much you can fit into ottoman divans/box springs, but look carefully at the storage space dimensions listed by the manufacturer, as there can be a surprising variation between similar-seeming examples.

The focus of any bedroom is, of course, the bed. Firstly, the best advice is to opt for the biggest one you can comfortably fit in your room – you'll need a minimum of approximately 60cm/2ft around it on each side, but ideally more (and remember that bedroom doors tend to swing inwards, so factor that into your calculations). Giving yourself – and your partner, if you have one – the largest possible amount of space to sleep in is a choice you'll never regret – especially if you start out as a couple, but end up with a family of kids who love to bed-hop!

If your room dimensions are tight, opt for a bed without a footboard – a storage divan/boxspring with drawers beneath or a lift-up mattress is a good choice, as the maximum dimensions of the bed tend to match the mattress size (plus you might be able to minimize other furniture in the room thanks to the bed's storage capacity). Alternatively, a neat, narrow bed frame with slim legs that has space underneath for storage boxes is another possibility that's worth exploring.

As a general rule of thumb, if you sleep on your side or change position a lot during the night, you'll be better off with a softer mattress, while those who sleep on their back are best served by a medium-firm design for lower back support. And the heavier you are, the firmer the mattress should be. But there's no substitute for trying out mattresses properly before you buy (spend at least 10 minutes lying on each one), and if you are sharing a bed, then make sure your partner is comfortable with it, too. You spend about a third of your life in bed, hopefully asleep, so it really is worth sourcing the right one for your needs.

It's usually pretty obvious where the bed should be positioned within a room, but if possible, make sure that the head of the bed is positioned away from any areas of noise or light.

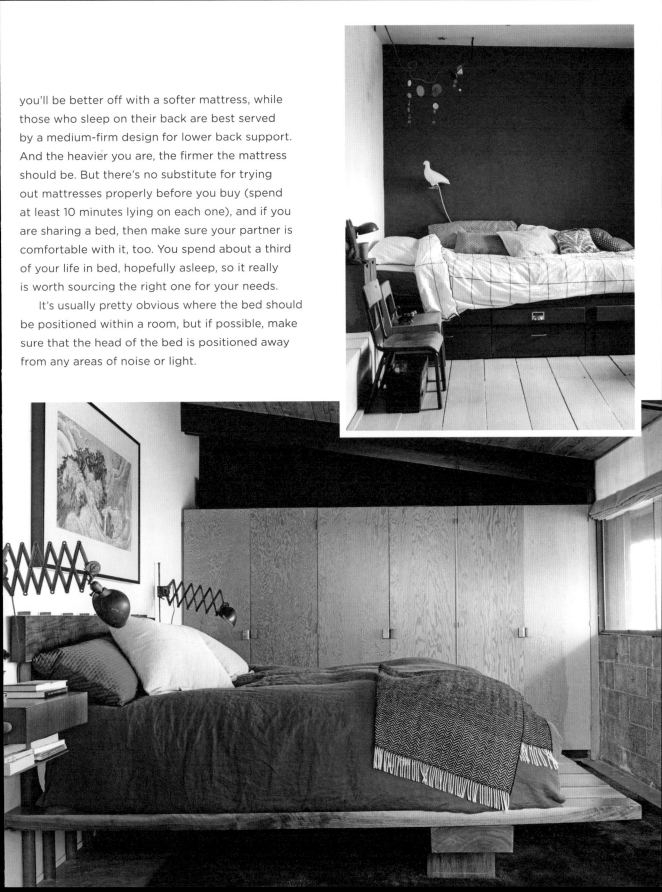

BATHING

Big or small, shared or en suite - bathrooms are perhaps the hardest-working spaces in the home. But as well as playing a functional role, bathrooms are also private places where we can relax and unwind, and their decor should reflect this aspect.

If you don't have the luxury of multiple bathrooms, it's essential that the one you have caters for every member of the family. If you're planning a new bathroom, you'll probably want to seek expert advice on technical issues such as water pressure and the position of the drainage pipes. Armed with that knowledge, you can move on to planning. Think how and when the space will be used and by whom. A busy family bathroom will need a durable, functional flooring such as rubber or vinyl, while an en suite shared by a couple would lend itself to something more luxe. If you'll all be jostling to use the bathroom in the morning, can you fit in two sinks, side by side? Don't limit yourself to one overhead light source. Two or three different fittings will allow you to switch mood from busy bathing zone to zen retreat (once the kids have gone to bed).

If space is tight, look at compact-sized tubs designed to have showers over them. Wall-hung basins and toilets create the illusion of a bigger floor space. Can you rehang the door so that it opens outwards, or fit a sliding door? If you're completely remodelling, then try to build as much storage as possible into the fabric of the room. And add as wall-mounted storage - this will make it easier to keep the family bathroom free of bath toys and teenage lotions and potions. A simple, pared-down aesthetic with light and reflective surfaces will visually expand the room.

SPA-STYLE BATHROOMS

PRACTICAL THINKING It's all very well emulating a spa aesthetic, but if the comfort levels don't stack up, then you won't feel the wellbeing benefits. As well as choosing fixtures carefully (slip off your shoes and climb into the tub in the showroom before making your selection, so you don't have to merely guess its lounging potential!), make sure you add practical accessories. A bathtub rack is a really useful addition, giving you somewhere to keep bath products, ambience-creating candles or even a glass of wine, close to hand while you soak (left and opposite).

Who wouldn't want to have a hotel or spa-style bathroom – somewhere soothing, calming and minimalist to start and end the day? The good news is that even the tiniest bathroom can be transformed into a calm, comforting retreat.

First of all, don't be deterred by an expanse of white tiles. A neutral palette is a great starting point and allows you to mix in colour and texture. Wood brings warmth to any interior, while subtle muted shades introduce a spa feel. Opt for plenty of matching fluffy white towels (wash on a hot cycle to keep them that way), roll them up and store in a basket. Towels in use can be hung on a towel rail or even a small towel ladder – easy to source nowadays. A slatted wooden or bamboo mat brings pleasing sauna vibes. Finally, house plants are not just for living rooms! Many varieties will thrive in the humid atmosphere of a bathroom, while quietly removing airborne pollutants and softening what can be quite a bland and clinical space.

KEEP ON DISPLAY!
Plants will transform your bathroom into a relaxing oasis – opt for ferns, peace lilies and palms, which all love high humidity and will thrive in a bathroom environment.

ROUGH LUXE Natural materials are perfect for creating an elegant and refined spa-like feel, but don't be afraid to use these in a slightly more rough-and-ready way – think 'tropical island beach' spa, rather than 'fancy urban hotel'. A minimalist approach with rustic materials and aged patinas balances style and practicality, and can be really easy to look after (this page and opposite).

EN-SUITE
BATHROOMS

Nowadays, an en-suite bathroom is an absolute
must-have for many of us, but a lot of older houses
were not built with even one indoor bathroom,
let alone more than one. This means that a little
creativity might be required in order to add en-suite
facilities to older homes. If your bedroom has a
built-in wardrobe/closet – and it's deep enough
– then you might want to look into whether it's
suitable for conversion into a shower enclosure.
Alternatively, if your budget will stretch, and an
adjoining room can be reduced in size, you could
steal a slice of the floor space and knock through
to create your en suite.

The other option is to bring the bathing facilities
into the bedroom itself – perhaps a freestanding
tub in the corner of the room (boutique hotel-
style), or a shower zone that's separated from the
sleeping area by a sheet of glass or a half-height

IN THE ZONE It's surprising how little space you
actually need for en-suite facilities – even a sliver
of space can be a functional bathroom if you use
a partition to separate the sleeping and bathing
areas, rather than a wall. Glazed partitions
help maintain a sense of space (above left and
right). However, owing to their lack-of-privacy
disadvantage, they're not for everyone! If your
budget will stretch to it, flip glass (which turns
opaque at the flick of a switch) might be ideal.

or full-height partition wall. If your room is big
enough, one configuration that works particularly
well is to have the bed positioned almost in the
middle of the room, with the headboard pushed
against a full-height partition wall (which only
stretches the width of the bed), and the en-suite
facilities or clothes storage neatly tucked away
behind that partition.

TAKE INSPIRATION
Keep a sense of synergy
between an en suite and the
bedroom it serves – here, the
coastal-inspired colour scheme
in the bathroom echoes the
bedroom decor perfectly.

CLEARING CLUTTER
IN THE BATHROOM

» Many homes have a bathroom that's barely big enough to include a toilet, sink and bathtub (perhaps with a shower over), with a medicine cabinet on the wall. This can make it pretty tricky to keep things neat and tidy – which, of course, is essential if you want to create the right ambience for a relaxing soak in the tub, and if you want to be able to clean speedily, too. The answer is to include a few pieces of small storage to keep toiletries and cleaning materials in order, as well as offer a place for towels and clothing to be hung.

» Hooks and rails should be your first thought – think about how many towels are in use at any one time, and make sure you have space for at least one more, preferably two to make it easier when you have guests to stay. If your DIY skills aren't up to drilling, then look at over-the-door hangers or suction-cup designs for an instant solution. Suction-cup shelves and other wall-hung storage also work particularly well as a quick fix for a tiny bathroom.

» Invest in a few large baskets – they are a good home for clean rolled-up towels waiting to be used as well as dirty towels and laundry. Their natural woven texture also enhances the decor, adding softness and contrast to all those shiny surfaces. Storage boxes or trays are a good choice for holding small items, not just because they streamline the aesthetics of shelves and windowsills, but because they make it easy to whizz everything out of the way when you need to clean. Just make sure the boxes are made from something durable and easy to clean, bearing in mind the damp, warm atmosphere of the bathroom.

KEEP IT CLEAN Bags and baskets are perfect for concealing bathroom clutter – but do make sure that they're suited to the bathroom environment. Natural fibres such as cotton and other plant-based materials including rush and wicker can become mouldy or mildewed if they stay damp for too long (opposite above left and below right). Your bathroom needs to be well ventilated in order to avoid this (an extraction fan should do the trick); if it's still a problem, opt for wooden items or even wipe-clean plastic, which will stand up better to the rigours of the humid environment (above and opposite).

SOURCE LIST

ONE-STOP

Crate & Barrel
crateandbarrel.com
Good furniture, lighting, homewares and practical storage options.

Dwell
dwell.co.uk
Furniture, storage and home accessories in a contemporary style.

Habitat
habitat.co.uk
Affordable modern design with retro touches.

Home Depot
homedepot.com
Storage solutions for the kitchen, laundry, craft room and garage.

IKEA
ikea.com
Famously affordable, functional Scandi design for every room.

John Lewis
johnlewis.com
Quality freestanding furniture, kitchens, lighting and storage solutions.

Pottery Barn
potterybarn.com
Wide selection of storage and homewares plus freestanding furniture.

Store
aplaceforeverything.co.uk
A useful resource for anyone sorting out their home's storage provision.

The Conran Shop
conranshop.co.uk
High-quality furniture, bed and table linens, lighting, home accessories and storage options.

The Holding Company
theholdingcompany.co.uk
Storage options galore, from drawer dividers to wall-mounted systems.

LIVING ROOM

Cox & Cox
coxandcox.co.uk
Contemporary furniture with a vintage edge, plus a few pieces with a more industrial vibe.

Graham & Green
grahamandgreen.co.uk
Quirkily designed products perfect for eclectic interiors, and those with a vintage, retro or industrial-chic edge.

Heal's
heals.co.uk
Designer contemporary and mid-century modern furniture and storage.

Lassco
lassco.co.uk
The place to go for ex-industrial pieces and architectural salvage.

Laura Ashley
lauraashley.com
Classically stylish furniture, including media units and bookshelves, plus chests of drawers and sideboards.

Leporello
leporello.co.uk
Hand-crafted painted furniture with French and Swedish influences.

Ligne Roset
ligneroset.com
Designer furnishings for contemporary living.

Made
made.com
Contemporary furniture and other homewares.

Marks & Spencer
marksandspencer.com
A choice of classic styles and edgier contemporary-looking pieces.

Norse Interiors
norseinteriors.com
Customize Ikea furniture with sleek Scandi-design doors, panels, drawer fronts and hardware.

Oka
oka.com
Beautiful freestanding furniture and other accessories.

Roche Bobois
roche-bobois.com
Achingly hip furniture for every room of the home.

The Old Cinema
theoldcinema.co.uk
Antique, vintage and retro furniture.

BEDROOM

Caravane
caravane.co.uk
Super-chic French homewares brand offering gorgeous textiles and home accessories.

Elfa
elfa.com
Wall-hung modular storage systems.

Go Modern
gomodern.co.uk
Contemporary bedroom furniture, including a wealth of storage beds.

Sweetpea & Willow
sweetpeaandwillow.com
French and Italian-inspired furniture, including trunks and blanket boxes.

The French Bedroom Company
frenchbedroomcompany.co.uk
Elegant, French-style bedroom furniture.

Furl
furl.co.uk
Specializes in storage beds that lift up to reveal a storage compartment.

KITCHEN

Chalon
chalon.com
Bespoke handmade kitchens plus furniture for bathrooms, bedrooms and dining rooms.

Crown Imperial
crown-imperial.co.uk
Kitchens plus fitted furniture for bedrooms and living spaces.

Ella's Kitchen Company
ellaskitchencompany.com
Nordic-style cabinets featuring dry pantries with retro food scoops for ingredient storage.

Greengate
greengate.dk
Cheerful vintage-style
small storage.

Lakeland
lakeland.co.uk
Storage solutions
for around the home.

BATHROOM

CP Hart
cphart.co.uk
Bathroom furniture in
a variety of styles, from
elegant to cutting edge.

Custom Fronts
customfronts.co.uk
Clean-lined kitchen fronts
made to fit standard Ikea
kitchen cabinets.

Ideal Standard
ideal-standard.co.uk
Clutter-concealing
bathroom furniture.

Kohler
kohler.com
US manufacturer of
bathroom vanity units
designed with the luxury
market in mind.

Porcelanosa
porcelanosa.com
Modern, minimalist
bathroom furniture as
well as designs with more
feminine, classic lines.

Roper Rhodes
roperrhodes.co.uk
Fitted furniture at a range
of affordable price points.

Scotts of Stow
scottsofstow.co.uk
Many options for beefing
up bathroom storage.

Topps Tiles
toppstiles.co.uk
The UK's biggest tile
specialist.

HALLWAY

The Cotswold Company
cotswoldco.com
Hallway storage furniture,
including shoe cabinets,
benches and coat racks.

The Dormy House
thedormyhouse.com
Painted furniture,
including a wealth of hall
storage options.

CHILDREN'S ROOMS

**Great Little Trading
Company**
gltc.co.uk
Child-specific furniture,
including play tables with
integrated drawers and
bins, and beds with
drawers and cupboards.

Stompa
stompa.com
Storage beds and
bedroom furniture.

Vertbaudet
vertbaudet.co.uk
Plenty of child-sized
storage options, including
toy bins, book caddies
and shoe tidies.

PICTURE CREDITS

al – above left / bl – bottom left / ar – above right / br – below right / m – middle; ; 1, 93 arl The London home of the interiors blogger Katy Orme (apartmentapothecary. com)/ph. Rachel Whiting; 2/3, 148–9 The home of Paul burgess and Karen Carter, designed by David Coote and Atlanta Bartlett, available for holiday lets and photography through www.beachstudios.co.uk/ph. Polly Wreford; 4 al, 95 ar The Brooklyn home of Asumi & Kuni Tomita of Kanorado Shop/ph. James Gardiner; 4 ar, 47, 70 Designer James van der Velden of Bricks Studio, Amsterdam/ ph. Benjamin Edwards; 5 al The Shack is available as a shoot location www.lordshippark.com/ ph. Benjamin Edwards; 5 ar Fred Musik/ ph. Debi Treloar; 6 The Brooklyn home of Martin Bourne and Leilin Lopez/ ph. Debi Treloar; 7 ar, 31 ar, 155 br Karine Kong, founder and Creative Director of online concept store BODIE and FOU, www.bodieandfou.com ph. Rachel Whiting; 7 bl CICO /ph. Helen Cathcart; 8/9, 16 al The summerhouse Of the fashion designer Charlotte Vadum in Denmark/ ph. Anna Williams; 10, 12/13 The home and shop of Katrina von Wowern of www.minaideer.se/ph. Rachel Whiting; 11 ar CICO /ph. Emma Mitchell and Penny Wincer; 11 bl Elaine Tian of Studio Joo/ph. James Gardiner; 14 The beach hideaway in Javea designed by Jessica Bataille www.jessicabatille.com/ph. Benjamin Edwards; 15, 16 bl, 24 bl Sasa Antic – Interior stylist, set and props/ph. Rachel Whiting; 16 br London home of Eloise Jones and Aine Donovan/ph. Catherine Gratwicke; 17, 26, 35 ar, 82, 103 bl, 158 Niki Brantmark of My Scandinavian Home/ph. Rachel Whiting; 18, 29 Victoria Smith, editor sfgirlbybay.com/ph. Rachel Whiting; 19, 34, 41 ar, 42 ar, 59, 102 Designed by Atlanta Bartlett and Dave Coote, available for hire through www.beachstudios.co.uk/ph. Polly Wreford; 20 al, 57 ar, 78 al, 138 al /ph. Debi Treloar; 20 bl Marina Coriasco/ph. Polly Wreford; 20 br, 166 al, 166 ar The home of the designer Anne Geistdoerfer (and her family) of double g architects in Paris/ ph. Catherine Gratwicke; 21, 28 al, 32, 54, 84 bl Anne Hubert designer of La Cerise sur le Gateau, www.lacerisesurlegateau. fr/ph. Rachel Whiting; 22 ar, 22 bl The home of the illustrator Kate Bingaman-Burt in Portland, Oregon/ph. Helen Cathcart; 23 The London home of the artist Bobby Petersen/ph. Katya de Grunwald; 24 ar, 25 bl, 94, 133 br, 143 ar, 143 bl Pauline's apartment in Paris, designed by Marianne Evennou www. marianne-evennou.com/ph. Rachel Whiting; 25 al, 138 al Home of Justine Hand, contributing editor at Remodelista, on Cape Cod/ph. Benjamin Edwards; 25 ar CICO /ph. Penny Wincer and Gavin Kingcome; 27, 141 br Designed by Armando Elias and Hugo D'Enjoy of Craft Design/ph. Rachel Whiting; 28 bl, 96 ar Jeska and Dean Hearne thefuturekept. com/ph. James Gardiner; 28 br, 33 br Artist and designer Sarah E. Owen/ph. Helen Cathcart; 30 ph. Andrew Wood/the home of Ellen Weiman & Dubi Silverstein in New York, designed by architects Ogawa/Depardon; 31 al CICO /ph. Emma Mitchell; 31 bl, 48 ar The family home of architect Arash Nourinejad and artist Kristina Lykke Tonnesen in Copenhagen/ph. Rachel Whiting; 33 al The home of Birgitte and Henrik Moller Kastrup in Denmark/ph. Rachel Whiting; 33 ar Alison Hill & John Taylor's home in Greenwich/ph. Jan Baldwin; 35 bl The home of the author/stylist Selina Lake/ph. Rachel Whiting; 36 al, 164 /ph. James Gardiner; 36 ar A family home in west London by Webb Architects and Cave Interiors/ph. Polly Wreford; 37 'Albany' in Port Isacc, designed by Nicola O'Mara and available to rent through www.boutique-retreats.co.uk/ph. Benjamin Edwards; 38, 60/61, 76, 153, 160 Susannah and David le Mesurier's home in Wales/ph. Rachel Whiting; 39, 113 bl, 114, 123 bl The home of Susanne Brandt and her family in Copenhagen/ph. Rachel Whiting; 40 The family home of designer and shop owner An-Magritt Moen in Norway/ph. Debi Treloar; 41 al The family home Lucy St George and Paul Batts of Rocket St George/ ph. Debi Treloar; 41 b The home of Katherine Jane Learmonth of www.cowboykate.co.uk in North Yorkshire/ph. Debi Treloar; 42 bl CICO /ph. Penny Wincer; 43 ar The family of Rebecca Proctor in Cornwall www.futurustricblog.com / ph. Rachel Whiting; 43 bl Indenfor & Udenfor in Copenhagen/ph. Polly Wreford; 44 The London home of the florist Fran Bailey of www.freshflower.co.uk/ph. Rachel Whiting; 45 al CICO /ph. James Gardiner; 45 am The home of Synne Skjulstad in Oslo/ ph. Catherine Gratwicke; 45 ar Dorthe Kvist garden and interior designer, stylist, TV host, blogger and author/ph. Katya de Grunwald; 46 al, 147 al The family home of Justina Blakeney in Los Angeles/ph. Rachel Whiting; 46 ar "La villa des Ombelles" the family home of Jean-Marc Dimanche, Chairmanof V.I.T.R.I.O.L. agency, www. vitriol-factory.com/ph. Debi Treloar; 46 br CICO /ph. James Gardiner; 48 al Rebecca Kierszbaum for Kierszbaum Interieurs/ph. Catherine Gratwicke; 49 Ylva Skarp ylvaskarp. se/ph. James Gardiner; 50, 152 al The home of interior journalist and blogger Jill Macnair in London/ph. Rachel Whiting ; 51, 62 al, 81, 136 br The West London home of Lou Rota, available to hire as a location/ph. Debi Treloar; 52 al The home of interior designer Tjimkje de Boer of tjimkje. com/ph. Catherine Gratwicke; 52 ar The family home of designers Alexandra and Nicolas Valla of Royal Roulette www.royalroulette.com/ph. Debi Treloar; 53 Designed by Atlanta Bartlett and Dave Coote, available for hire through www.beachstudios.co.uk/ph. Polly Wreford; 55 al Jonathan Lo/ph. Rachel Whiting; 55 ar The South London home of Carole Poirot of www.mademoisellepoirot.com/ph. Rachel Whiting; 55 bl, 88 al The family home of David Cowling and Tara Bell/ph. Debi Treloar; 57 bl, 133 bl The Philadelphia home of Kristian Lazzaro/ph. Debi Treloar; 62 bl The family home of Quentin Leroux in Paris, designed by Royal Roulotte www.royalroulotte/ph. Debi Treloar; 63, 130 The family home of Alison Smith in Brighton/ph. Polly Wreford; 64, 79, 162, 169 al The family home of Gina Portman of Folk at Home www.folkathome.com/ph. Catherine Gratwicke; 65 al CICO / ph. Simon Brown; 65 ar The home of Shelley Carline, owner of the shop Hilary and Flo in Sheffield/ph. Debi Treloar; 65 br The home of Stephanie Zak in London/ph. Debi Treloar; 66/67 The home of James Lynch and Sian Tucker of fforset. bigcartel.com and coldatnight.co.uk/ph. James Gardiner; 68 al The home of Grant and Sam, owners of Petite Violette in Malmo, Sweden/ph. Rachel Whiting; 68 ar The home of garden designer and author Dorthe Kvist meltdesignstudio.

com/ph. Rachel Whiting; 70 bl CICO /ph. James Gardiner; 71 Tina B/ph. Debi Treloar; 72 al The home of Jonathan Sela and Megan Schoenbachler/ph. Catherine Gratwicke; 72 ar The family home of designers Ulla Koskinen & Sameli Rantanen in Finland/ph. Debi Treloar; 72 bl CICO /ph. James Gardiner; 73, 74-75, 128, 141 al The home of Marie Emilsson www. trip2garden.se /ph. Rachel Whiting; 77 bl The family home of Jane Rocket and Toby Erlam of Rockett St George/ph. Catherine Gratwicke ; 77 ar Stella Willing stylist/designer and owner of house in Amsterdam/ph. Debi Treloar; 78 ar Workstead/ph. Pia Ulin; 80 Interior design by Beth Dadswell of inperfectinteriors.co.uk/ph. Rachel Whiting; 83 al, 95 bl The home of Desiree of VosgesParis.com/ph. Rachel Whiting; 83 ar CICO /ph. James Gardiner; 83 bl The family home of Paola Sells of www.sugarkids.es in Barcelona/ph. Rachel Whiting; 84 ar Ben Pentreath's London office/ph. Jan Baldwin; 85 the guesthouse of the interior designer & artist Philippe Guilmin, Brussels/ph. Debi Treloar; 86, 92, 93 bl The home of Jane Schouten of All the Luck in the World blog/ph. Rachel Whiting; 87 ar, 89 Chloe Thurston Instagram.com/ chloeuberkid, uberkid.net/ph. Ben Robertson; 87 bl The home of designer and author Anna Joyce in Portland, Orgeon/ph. Helen Cathcart; 88 bl, 125 bl The home of the Ponsa-Hemmings family of xo-inmyroom.com/ph. Rachel Whiting; 90, 120 ar The home of Ashlyn Gibson, founder of children's concept store Olive Loves Alfie, interior stylist/ writer and children's fashion stylist/ph. Rachel Whiting/ph. Rachel Whiting; 91 al, 105, 108, 117 ar The home of Nici Zinell, designer of Noe & Zoe in Berlin, and Knut Hake, film editor/ ph. Rachel Whiting; 91 ar The Fried family home in London/ ph. Winfried Heinze; 93 br The Paris home of designer Myriam de Loor, owner of Petit Pan/ph. Debi Treloar; 96 al The home in Copenhagen of designer Birgitte Raben Olrik of Raben Saloner/ph. Polly Wreford; 97 Tracy Wilkinson www. twworkshop.com/ph. Catherine Gratwicke; 98 Sophie Eadie's family home in London/ph. Jane Baldwin; 99 www. styleclusief.nl/ph. Catherine Gratwicke; 100/101, 111 br, 125 ar, 126-7, 140 Agata Hamilton www.my-home.com.pl/ph. Ben Robertson; 103 ar, 151 bl Oliver Heath and Katie Weimer – sustainable architecture, interior and jewellery design/ph. Catherine Gratwicke; 104 al The home of Sabien Engelenburg, the founder/designer of engelpunt.com/ph. Rachel Whiting; 104 bl, 117 bl, 136 bl The family home of Louise and Garth Jennings in London/ph. Rachel Whiting; 106/7 The family home of the designer Nina Nagel of byGraziela.com/ph. Ben Robertson; 109 al, 120 al, 123 br The family home of Francesca Forcolini and Barry Menmuir, designers and co-founders of fashion label Labour of Love/ ph. Ben Robertson; 109 bl The Clapton Laundry – available for photographic shoots, boutique events and creative workshops/ph. Ben Robertson; 109 br Een Schoon Oog – interior design and styling by Sonja de Groot/ph. Ben Robertson; 110 Anki Wijnen & Casper Boot of www. zilverblauw.nl & www.jahallo.nl/. Rachel Whiting; 111 al Kristina Dam Studio/ph. James Gardiner; 111 bl Elle & Aarrons' rooms on Riverbank, Hampton Court/ph. Winfried Heinze; 112 Monika of Kaszka.Mlekiem.com, co-founder of girlsontiptoes. com/ ph.Ben Robertson; 113 ar, 115 The home of Nadine Richter, designer and co-owner of Noe & Zoe in Berlin/ph.

Rachel Whiting; 116 The home of Britt, Jurgen and Mascha/ ph. Rachel Whiting; 117 al Swedish mamma of four living in Leigh-on-sea, with Ralph/ ph.Ben Robertson; 118 The family home of the architects Jeanette and Rasmus Frisk of www. arkilab.dk/ ph.Ben Robertson; 119 The family home of Camilla Ebdrup of LUCKYBOYSUNDAY/ph. Rachel Whiting; 121 The family home of Louise Kamman Riising, co-owner of hey-home.dk/ph. Rachel Whiting; 122 Malgosia Jakubowska, ladnebebe.pl/ph. Ben Robertson; 125 al, 171 The family home of Aneta of Lola y Lolo in Poland/ph. Ben Robertson ; 129 ar architect William Smalley's London flat/ph. Jan Baldwin; 129 bl The home of Leida Nassir-Pour of Warp & Weft in Hastings/ph. Claire Richardson; 131 The family home of Sara Duchars of craft kit company www.buttonbag.co.uk and photographer Dan Duchars/ ph. Debi Treloar; 132 al, 145 The Paris apartment of Thierry Dreano, designed by the architect Sylvie Cahen/ph. Rachel Whiting; 132 b Home of architect Reinhard Weiss & Bele Weiss in London/ph. Polly Wreford; 134 Kimberley Austin of Austin Press, San Francisco/ph. Helen Cathcart; 135 ar The home of decorator Bunny Turner of www.turner pocock.co.uk/ph. Polly Wreford; 135 br, 159 ar The home of Virginie Denny, fashion designer and Alfronso Valles, painter/ph. Debi Treloar; 136 al The home and studio of the artist/stylist Inge Cremer in the Netherlands/ph. Helen Cathcart; 136/7 ar The London home of producer James Watersand floral design and photographer Yolanda Chiaramello www.choppywaters.com and www.chiaramello. co.uk/ph. Debi Treloar; 137, 161 ar The cabin of Hanne Borge and her family in Norway/ph. Catherine Gratwicke; 138 ar The Paris apartment of Audree Chabert, designed by the architect Sylvie Cahen/ph. Rachel Whiting; 139 An artist's house in the Netherlands/ ph. Rachel Whiting; 141 ar Judith Kramer, owner of webshop Juudt.com; the art of living; living and art/ph. Polly Wreford; 142 designer Helen Ellery's home in London/ph. Jan Baldwin; 143 al, 144 br Designed by Stephane Garotin and Pierre Emmanuel Martin Hand in Lyon/ ph. Rachel Whiting; 144 al Textile designer and founder of Missemai, missemai.com/ ph. Ben Robertson; 144 bl CICO / ph. James Gardiner; 146, 176 The house of Eugenie and Olivier in Brussels/ph. Debi Treloar; 147 ph. Debi Treloar; 150 The London home of the interiors blogger Kety Orme (apartmentapothecary.com)/ph. Rachel Whiting; 151 ar, 156 ar Myriam Balay www.myriambalay.fr/ph. Debi Treloar; 152 ar Rebecca Uth, creator of Ro/ph. James Gardiner; 154 Home of Tim Rundle and Glynn Jones/ph. Debi Treloar; 155 bl /ph. Hans Blomquist; 157 'Nautilis' is the home in Cornwall of James and Lisa Bligh www.uniquehomestays.com/ph. Benjamin Edwards; 159 b The Los Angles home of Gina Blackman, www.blackmancruz.com/ph. Catherine Gratwicke; 161 bl Apifera, a stone cottage in Herefordshire available to rent through uniquehomestays.com/ph. Rachel Whiting; 163 The Brooklyn loft of Alina Preciado, owner of lifestyle store Dar Gitane www.dargitane.com/ph. Polly Wreford; 165 www. stylexclusive.nl/ph. Catherine Gratwicke; 167, 168 The Old Coastguard House – home of Martin and Jane Will/ph. Benjamin Edwards; 169 ar The seaside home of designer Marta Nowicka, available to rent/ ph. Rachel Whiting; 169 bl CICO /ph. Mark Scott; 169 br The Norrmans Boutique B&B, Denmark/ ph. Rachel Whiting

INDEX

ACKNOWLEDGMENTS

Thank you to all my friends and family who put up with my fretting about wordcounts and deadlines, and kept me on track when I got distracted by my own ideas and was tempted to start decorating rather than focus on the writing job in hand! And massive thanks must go to the wonderful team at RPS — to Annabel, for giving me the opportunity to tackle the kind of down-to-earth interiors book project I love; to Megan, for her beautiful layouts; and to everyone else who was involved in bringing this book to fruition.